Obadiah Cyrus Auringer

The Voice of a Shell

Obadiah Cyrus Auringer

The Voice of a Shell

ISBN/EAN: 9783743308169

Manufactured in Europe, USA, Canada, Australia, Japa

Cover: Foto ©Thomas Meinert / pixelio.de

Manufactured and distributed by brebook publishing software
(www.brebook.com)

Obadiah Cyrus Auringer

The Voice of a Shell

SATCHEL SERIES.

THE

Voice

of a

Shell.

PRICE 40 CENTS.

THE

VOICE OF A SHELL.

BY

O. C. AURINGER.

NEW YORK:
THE AUTHORS' PUBLISHING COMPANY,
BOND STREET.

CONTENTS.

WHEREFORE.

OLD minstrel ocean hath a hundred harps,
Hanging in niches on the mossy walls
Of his resplendent coral palaces,
Down in his mystic kingdom of the deep.
Some, in the silence of perpetual sleep,
Are mouldering away in idleness,
Corroding with the damps of centuries,
With no soul to recall their melody,
Since Superstition fled the near approach
Of scornful cold-eyed science, and became
A forlorn haunter of forgottem tombs,
In empires smouldering through unfruitful years.
And there are others whose sweet minstrelsy

(5)

Shall never falter. These the wanderer hears
Breathe through the silence of his ocean dream,
Mingled and indistinct, but powerful
To sooth to slumber or exalt to song.
Their's is the strain that summons to the dance,
In shell-paved halls, the ministers of mirth;
To glad the hearts of ocean deities,
With their rich prodigality of charms—
To drop a pictured curtain o'er their cares—
A waving wall of pantomimic shapes
Before the fading figures of their woes,
And with the mingled charm of sights and sounds
Woo them into the realm of fantasy.
But there is one whose wild and warlike note
Startles the echoes of his empire round,
Hushing at once the myriad voices raised
In long resounding peals of merriment—
The harp of war, which marshals in his realm
The headlong warriors of his bold phalanx,

Arrayed for marches through aerial fields,

To meet the skurrying legions of the winds,

Shaking white terror from their tossing crests,

With shouts that jar the lofty firmament,

And make the soft stars veil their darling eyes

Behind their tumbling barrier of clouds.

The sailor hears the warning from afar,

And speeds his poor ship to protecting bays

With white wings flung aloft in fleecy folds,

Skimming the brine like osprey on the wing ;

And if o'erta'en in the unequal race

Close-reefs his sails and bravely meets the brunt

Of elemental war, and rides it out,

Or drifts a wreck along the tempest's track.

If I have snatched a passing note from thee,

O stern and troublous spirit of the deep,

O wild and boistrous singer of the sea,

And caged it in imagination's haunt

Till it hath grown a free and fearful thing,

Sometimes to cheer, but oft to torture me—
To torture me with restless wrestlings long,
And sudden thrills and rages—cold sea fears,
And all a strange soul's strange anxieties,
Then I must often sing in its conceit,
For silence when it speaks is maddening:
So rise, mysterious spirit, when thou wilt,
And I will raise my voice to quiet thee!

THE VOICE OF A SHELL.

TEMPEST AND DESTINY.

A PANORAMA.

I.

A FEARFUL night! by Jove, a furious night!
The storm harps of the world have struck a strain,
Assembling nature's warriors to the field
Of their dread tourney on the heaving breast
Of a storm troubled ocean, there to tilt
Their fiery lances in the face of heaven,
And clang their armor in her startled ears!
Hark how the arm̀ed echo of the shock
Runs rattling down the sounding halls of night!
Behold old Neptune, wakened by the sound,
Heave back the curtains of his moving couch
And shake his gray locks on the hurricane!
Hear the hoarse murmur of his awful voice,
Proclaiming revel through his drowsy halls
As he partakes of passion's stirring wine—

Halloing to the keepers of his chase
To loose his pack of terror-throated dogs
To bay the mad game down his long arcades!
The row is rife; all powers save that of earth,
And she awe-struck and silent, join the rout,
Roar, rage and clamor with defiant lungs,
Swing their puissant arms and shriek full hoarse,
And mingle and contend in mad melee.
A furious night! by Jove, a fearful night!

II.

Look, where a solitary being stands,
Upon the top of yon high-lifted crag,
Whose base is stormed at by the yelling seas,
Whose brow is set against the worrying winds,
Whose scarred and bony bosom fronts the whole!
As the last hero of a perished race—
The lonely remnant of a giant race—
Lifts his grim front among a thousand foes,
And lets them rave their feeble lives away,
In calm, heroic grandeur looking far
Out o'er their heads into another land,
Beyond the thick and curdled horizon,
Whither the grand hope of his soul has flown.
Upon his withered brow the figure stands,
With head erect and strong arms calmly crossed

Upon a bosom of athletic breadth;
Like work of art struck from the solid cliff,
Wrought to adorn its native solitude,
And mock the rude destroyer at its feet.
Mark the expression on that marble face,
Full-set in its dark frame of falling hair.
And then the look in those stern steadfast eyes,
So eloquent of deep devouring thoughts.
A shadow rests upon that lofty brow,
White as sea-surf, and bared before the sweep
Of the swift tempest's wings, as if within
Its alabaster walls a creature sleeps,
That he would fain awaken and set free.
Now buried in impenetrable gloom
The figure with its aspect is unseen,
As the dark curtain falls on all, o'er all—
A quick and awful heaping up of gloom.
Here we, pure chainless spirits, will abide—
We, boundless roamers of eternal wilds,
And plains, and floods, and strange chaotic wastes,
Who once had mortal bonds, and sometimes turn
From heavenly paths to look upon old scenes,
And watch the ones who wander in the shade
And shadow of this fluctuating sphere;
Though while we mingle with the things of earth,

We don again the earth's infirmities.
Yes, here we'll hover in the tempest's time,
And watch this mortal till the tragic chain
That lies coiled up within his darkling mind
Becomes unwound by language or by act,
And shows the dusky splendor of his dreams.
No sailor man upon his high look-out,
Though clad in raiment rough and simple, he;
No ready watchful attitude is his,
Like one who bends at every brilliant flash
His piercing glance athwart the raging night,
Far out to sea.   A spirit of the time,
Companion of the storm, or part of it;
Or some ill-omen'd bird of night seems he,
Perched on his eyrie, high and desolate,
With eyes that note his victim's gambolings
In the dread moment that precedes the spring.
Look once again! the set of that white face
Has melted in the presence of a smile,
Which mounts the fine lip with a breathing scorn,
And seems half bitter by the dancing light
Of heaven's far-piercing, all-discerning eye!
But hush, he speaks—the storm not wholly drowns
The ringing intonations of that voice,
At once as steady and as passionate

As some shrill bugle playing to the winds!
" Wrecks, lightnings, thunders and earth-shaking seas!
Fierce joy and terror join in mutual war
And make the sea and sky their battle fields,
Charging their gusty legions o'er the land
As if to hold the hearts of man in awe,
And teach how poor his grandest passions are.
All men, I mean, save me; I cannot fear
What have been my companions since the hour
That brought the light of consciousness to me—
Companions I have loved and still must love
While this brain holds its melancholy guest,
And this heart burns with energy divine!
Hear how they roar around this gray old crag,
Which they have pounded these five thousand years,
But all in vain; for firm as at his birth
His feet stand steadfast planted in the flood,
His proud head held erect among the clouds.
My soul's at home in this wild company;
In their fierce natures dwells a sympathy—
A kinder love for my old brooding thoughts
Than the cold manner of mankind betrays.
There is a glory in this god-like strife,
An exhibition of sublimest strength
That wakes an antique spirit in my breast.

And makes me feel that I have some time known,
Back in the gloom of the heroic past,
Another being and a nobler life,
Compared with which this dim existence seems
The fleeting phantom of abnormal dreams.
'Tis but a flash—a momentary gleam
Shooting across the closed abyss of time,
Lighting a breath these crumbling walls of clay—
A transient ray, but oh, more eloquent
Of what concerns the soul's vast destiny
Than all the world's profound philosophy!
A golden link in that enormous chain
Which binds our being with the vast sublime,
And up whose submerged sections now we grope,
Watching for glintings of the upper day.
Grand and complete it looks to angel eyes,
Girdling the forehead of the Infinite—
The thread on which creation's gems are strung,
Strung like the pearls upon a beauty's brow,
The dazzling spheres in due gradation placed
As mounts the gradual scale of excellence.
But viewed by medium of human ken
It seems but fragmentary—incomplete.
Life is too short, and man too blind to trace
Its subtle windings or compute its scope;

Only a little glimmer now and then
Of precious light reveals its lustrous coil,
A little length, wound in life's bottom sands,
In light or shadow, as the fickle glass
Through which we view things is serene or foul,
Clear or obscure as pain-waves ebb or flow.
Would that my nature, like these elements,
Could grant a respite after every strife,
Could let calm peace succeed the rage of hell,
'Stead of the cold return to joyless gloom,
The doors of which yawn to receive me back,
As dungeon doors gape for the prisoner
While he toils fiercely 'neath the master's lash.
Oh, for some lovely loving human heart
Of which to make my hope's firm anchorage!
A haven for my life's far-wandering bark
To rest in when the hot typhoon is spent!
That I might taste of love, and tasting live,
As others in God's glorious sunlight breathe,
Blessing and blessed through the long gladsome years,
Which bring their little cares, but heaps of love,
And hope and sweet companionship, all crowned
With a fair faith and hope in bliss beyond—
In glorious vistas opening up beyond—
Toward which they move with step unfaltering.

How far from such is this loose dream of mine,
Broken and disconnected, winding on
In deep obscurity, but flashing out
At intervals a broad and brilliant flame,
Hot and vehement! instantaneous scenes
Thrown 'gainst a background of the deepest black,
Betraying in a single pulse of time
What should be gathered by the toil of years.
Still 'tis *some* joy to know that I exist,
Since this existence is the strangest thing—
The maddest thing of all conceivèd things—
The climax of all unreality!
For is that real which so soon dissolves,
And is at once as if it ne'er had been?
But yesterday, a pale and trembling star
Set on a reef amidst the breakers' reel;
To-day, a beacon on a storm-jarred rock,
Warring and fierce, while drop by drop the oil
Wastes from the vessel, and without, the shock—
The tireless strokes of strong determined foes—
Threaten its instant everlasting fall;
To-morrow—where, among the wrecks of things
May its storm-sundered, sad remains be found?
It cannot be! reality assumes
No such unstable, *ignis fatuus* proof,

But owns a self distinct from dull decay :
Else why this impulse ever reaching up,
And pushing onward, onward eagerly,
Toward something that e'er eludes the grasp?
The primary stage of universal truth,
Its past a life of god-like innocence;
The infant state of our progressive life,
With death the door to an advanced degree—
The threshold of a higher, more complete;
Thus on o'er paths that ever upward tend,
The soul unsatisfied pursues its way,
Drinking from purer fountains as it goes,
Until the mind, prepared, can calmly view
Creation's majesty from God's own star.
Such, something tells me, is the way and end
Of those who dare to combat and to soar;
And I am fain to heed that inner voice,
That sings its song in spite of the tumult
For aye endeavoring to drown it down,
Believing only in reality
As it exists in some last perfect state.
But quite enough of this philosophy,
Which tends but to the mind's bewilderment;
As vain as all such word-philosophies,
Springing in speculative idleness

From soils drained of all vital nourishment—
Plants of gigantic growth, but void of sap,
Or pith or sinew, but where sweet birds sing
Some thrilling songs a little while and die,
As constitutional decay creeps up
With secret progress through the poisoned veins,
Till branch by limb the vast illusion sinks
And sudden falls, as rotten empires fall,
Crumbling to naught before the rising sun
Of some long-suffering and patient soul,
Whose work is grounded on the lives of men;
Yes, quite enough of this philosophy—
And yet methinks it suits right well the hour,
Which is brimful of desperate conceits!
Men have gone mad by feasting on such fruit,
And it was just! for man is formed to act,
Using his fancy as a medium
To fuse his several gifts, thus forming one
Grand combination and harmonious whole
Of elements ordained susceptible
Of union by the will's cute chemistry—
A wall of equal strength to break the foe.
In vain he plunges in that seething lake
Whose tide returns but wrecks unto the shore—
That depth of speculation which confounds

The powers and breeds uncertain fantasies !
Here will I check my life's too careless course,
And train it to strong action's thoroughfare.
Let this suffice : a beacon will I build,
Under the base of yon projecting rock,
Whose gray head leans attentive o'er the edge
Of the bold precipice, as if to note
If the rude sea encroach on his domain.
Its light will be more constant than the flame
Of quick-dissolving lightnings of the sky.
There, where grim wreckers in the by-gone times
Reared funeral piles to children of the sea,
Will I, almost as fierce of heart as they,
Heap up the funereal pyre of fantasy,
And watch the pale ghosts of my many ills
Arise in smoke and dissipate in night."

And still the reckless revel rattles on !

III.

WHAT, has the night-bird quit his airy roost ?
His cry has ceased to wail along the storm ;
We hear the old winds howl in epic rage,
As if to rouse the stolid rocks to hear ;
And as if in some iron vault beneath,
An uncouth beast stalks restless to and fro,

Growling his discontent, we hear the waves
Roaring and snarling in their vicious way,
But not a human voice mixed in with them.
Watch till the eye of night again unclose
To view the desperation of the scene.
Ah, there it dances, and the owl is there,
Still brooding—brooding—in his loneliness;
Still groping in his mind's dim cabinet
For the lost source of fancy's fickle star,
With eyes on which the light of joy falls dead—
Shines dead as moonbeam on a stagnant pool,
So long have old illusions fed their sight.
Yet we must love this strong impassioned soul—
This wild enraptured poet of the heart,
Whose song moves with the measure of the winds,
And moves with woe the heavy ear of heaven!
Hark! there his sad complainings go again,
Swelling the howling chorus of the gods!
"I cannot move—I cannot act—my brain
Seems burning up, and on my bosom's throne
A bitter spirit has presumed to sit,
And taunt me with the melancholy there!
But let him sneer; my torch shall scare him hence,
Back to his dreary dungeon in the ground;
While *she* shall see its glimmer from her room,

And pity me my utter wretchedness!
She pity me! How quick my bosom's fiend
Ceases his scoffing when I think of her,
Whose love would change the tenor of my dreams,
And throne an angel where a demon sits!
Oh what a mine of love lies in this breast,
Beneath its ever working mass of care.
Oh, what a throng of glorious desires
Sleeps in this clouded temple of the joys,
Repressed by stern misfortune's icy hand!
O lone and melancholy, loved by none;
O lone and melancholy, loving still—
Most fondly her who cannot feel a touch
Of aught more strong than pity in her breast,
For one whose brain is maddening for her love;
For one whose heart is wilting for her smile;
For one who snatched from the devouring waves
Her precious life, one night just such as this;
When the wan reaper stalked sublimely forth
To gather in his harvest on the deep,
And heaven was burdened with the cries of men
Torn wrestling from their little hold of life,
To find a port in some lone coral cave,
While wrath and wreck were orders of the hour.
Would I had perished at the very time

That saw her safe, ere she had quit my arms,
In whose embrace she cold and dripping lay,
So pale and limber that I thought her dead ;
While the sweet kiss with which I called her back
To consciousness yet thrilled my being's core,
Waking a bliss I had not known before.
Then I had done a worthy thing indeed,
And she, perhaps, would hold my memory dear—
More dear for dying in her dear defence,
Than living but to make my madness known.
But when I ponder, oft I laugh perforce—
E'en in the moment of sharp agony ;
Laugh with a glee spasmodically wild—
A humor overpowering and absurd,
To recognize in this absurdest mood
The night-hawk's passion for the turtle-dove.
Was ever anything so fondly vain ?
Was love ever wed with folly like to this ?
For who could love a creature of my sort—
A dreamer of strange dreams, whose gaiety
Was not that fascinating flow of joy
Which certain natures have inherited—
That magnet which attracts in restless throngs
The shallow votaries of void conceits,
And holds a power which but too oft usurps

The noble place assigned to honest worth,
Winning an angel to true love's despair!
Mine was a mirth most silent and most deep,
And full of ecstacy both deep and still—
The music of a heart too wildly strung,
Fed on imaginative fruit too young.
A haunter of old mouldering ruins, I,
Where the owl mourned the prostrate centuries;
A frequenter of ancient battle fields
Spread out beneath the still watch of the stars,
Forming in waking dreams the warlike ghosts
Of the old armies that contended there,
Into live regiments, brigades and squads,
And marching them in chivalrous array
To battle for imaginary fair;
Watching the wild flow of their shadowy flags,
Led to the charge upon the frightened wind,
And fancying each gust the dying shout
Of many stricken heroes in their pain;
Feeling the hot whirl of attack and rout,
Skirmish, retreat and rally and deploy,
Gyrating round me as I sat entranced—
Strung with heroic energy the while,
The rapt director of two destinies.
Then, when the cloud of chimeric war passed off,

And every armed ghost gone at my command,
I gathered relics from the haunted sea
To treasure up as miser does his gold,
To dream and ponder o'er in solitude.
Was this a picture for a girlish heart,
O'erflowing with love's romance and desire,
To treasure up apart from everything
Within its inmost secret solitude?
Yet I was happy, strangely happy then,
When suddenly, the vision of that face,
Dawning like sunburst on my desert path,
Burst up a smouldering mountain in my breast,
Damming the current of my life's still stream,
Rolling its volumes back upon my heart,
There to ferment and boil within the heat
Of that volcano's unrestricted wrath.
Not since that time has lovely peace essayed
To brave the inner tempest and resume
The throne she was constrained to abdicate.
The temple where she held her glittering court,
With all its vast and varied pageantry;
Its dreamy halls, intoxicating heights,
Its opening vistas, winy atmosphere,
The glory of its fairy summer-land
Is now a ruin where all black shapes flit,

Cradle of whirlwinds and all furious things;
A waste of twisted labyrinthine ways—
O'ergrown and dangerous, treacherous maze—
Through which my winged thoughts are doomed to rush
Without the hope of reaching any gaol!
Enough! I'll dream no more, but bravely act,
Though in the acting I go wholly mad!
Shall I go mad? a fearful question, that,
Involving every horror, fear, disgust—
All that is loathesome to the heart of man.
Why does that cold appalling terror rise
So oft of late to shake me like a leaf
Struck by an icy current from the north?
Because I hear it whispered in my ear
By some persistent little fiend of hell—
' Mad as the storm, in storm thy star shall set.'
Enough! such thoughts I'll entertain no more,
Though they be prophets of unerring tongue!
In vain the contest, so I'll kindle up
The holacaust of spirits such as they."

    Starting with cautious motion from his stand,
With feeling steps he gropes along the crag,
And down a steep declivity to where
A little cave the lightning has revealed
Sunk in the bony bosom of the earth,

A ragged wound torn in the giant's ribs,
From which a pile of fuel he brings forth,
And clambers down a long descent with it,
O'er boulders black and burnt that scattered lie,
Where thunderbolts have hurled them from on high ;
And chasms that 'mong the splintered ruins lurk,
To trap the careless footstep in the dark.
Placing his heavy burden at the foot
Of an o'ertopping tower of adamant,
Whose leaning form make a protected space
Of many feet under its even base,
He forms the whole into a pyramid,
In which he thrusts a miniature brand.
Forth from the dry mass darts a little spark,
Which leaps and rises to a stalwart fiend
That stretches fiery fingers forth for food ;
A crimson flame upon the crest of night,
Waving the hovering shadows o'er the brink
Of the tremendous downright precipice ;
Warming the rugged rocks with ruddy glow,
And faintly touching up the scene below.

And still the furious can-can rattles on !

IV.

Oh ! 'tis a fearful thing for man to feel
The fatal gift of genius in his breast !

That dread prerogative, creative power,
Whose influence scathes all that it breathes upon;
To hear that voice imperative within
Forever crying for mysterious things,
In language like the worrying of guilt—
A language that hath no interpreter;
To feel the burning furnace of the brain
Mould of its heaped-up mass a living life,
To move expansive through immensity,
Mocking the deadly pride that gave it birth!
Oh, the fierce cravings of that prisoner,
Who caged in flesh doth rend his prison house
With harpy instincts uncontrollable!
Whose giant size demands a wider scope—
A boundless pleasure field in which to build,
Alone, unheeded, wedded to his strength,
Cramped in his dungeon walls of wasting clay,
He makes a hideous hell of his confines
In the o'erstrong necessity for war
Inseparable from those chaotic souls
Which build on ruins their immortal fames.

The watcher stands with sad and dreamy eye
Fixed on the beacon's fluctuating flare,
As if he traces in its glowing heart

Passions like those that mutilate his own,
And watches calmly to behold the end.
" In vain ! I see how mad is the attempt
To stay the onward current of my fate,
Which bears me on and on, I know not where.
Now do I learn at last the latent truth
That I have ever pinched myself in vain
With scruples idle as the idlest thing ;
How useless 'tis to battle with these foes,
Whose pride will suffer no competitors ;
That nothing which the Infinite has fixed
May be combatted, questioned or defined,
But all accepted with humility,
Chaff with the wheat, dross with the precious ore
'Till Time shall sift and separate the heap.
I am like one of those mysterious wrecks
Which sailors tell of with a shrinking awe,
Seen on white midnights far as southern seas,
Forever drifting—drifting ceaselessly ;
No mortal hand to work the idle wheel
Or trim the sails to every veering breeze ;
Impelled by secret currents of the waste
Of dim confused distracted elements.
They tell of voices sad and wondrous sweet
Rising at times from their deserted holds,

Of songs that steal the listening seas along,
Filling the void of night with melody—
That haunts forevermore the listener's soul,
And sometimes, too, as one stalks silent by,
Flooded with ghastly waves of lunar light,
A rippling laugh floats through the hollow ports,
And the hull shakes with ghastly merriment,
As if a band of ghouls held revel there;
Again, a single desolating cry,
Followed by low complainings, may be heard,
And then the rotting hulk steals slowly by—
And disappears upon the horizon—
Crumbling away upon the horizon,
Gone, as it came upon them, like a dream.
Such are the mysteries that make my life
An exhibition for the curious,
And me an object to be pointed at—
A mark for fools to aim their arrows at!
I am the wretched slave of wayward sprites,
Who make my faculties the vehicle
To bear their foibles through the ways of men!
Reft of all power to act my own resolves,
I feel their cutting reins direct my course,
Forcing me o'er an ever shifting way.
I little reck how it may terminate—

'Tis a condition I have come to loathe,
This singing, singing my old wailing songs,
The weary, weary songs that never cease,
The same old weary wailings o'er and o'er.
Welcome such change as comes to liberate,
Be it as mirth or madness, anything—
E'en death, so it but brings oblivion
To fold his cloudy mantle o'er all."

A charge of Titans overpowers the voice
Of the sad singer of the solitude.
But hark! above the infernal worrying
Of their far failing voices, inland borne,
A lithe light footstep rings upon the rock,
And a fair girlish form, wrapped in the folds
Of a dark sea-cloak, pauses at his side;
A lovely hand throws back a sheltering hood,
Letting a cataract of tresses fall
Around a bust of perfect symmetry;
A face of loveliness most exquisite,
With eyes that look things all unspeakable
From their impassioned darkly brilliant depths,
Glows in the firelight strangely animate,
Flushed and vivacious with pure exercise.
With parted lips of love and fluttering breath,

Sweet as the breath of winds from fairy isles,
She stands like some dear angel of the spheres
Sent on a mission of humanity!

One rapid glance the startled watcher throws
Upon this lovely vision of the night,
With sudden exclamation crying out—
"You, Mora, here in such a storm as this?
What can have brought you out at such a time!
Has aught occurred at home to fetch you here,
Flying like sweet ghost on a warrior's watch?
Speak quick, or I shall think your spirit come
To warn me of some unexpected harm!"

"Grant me but time to catch my breath again,
And I will prove to you I am no ghost,
Although I've taken their proverbial hour
To venture out into this dreadful storm.
No—no—nothing unusual has occurred—
Pa has departed for the Mangrove Beach
Against the tempest to secure the boats;
I could not rest alone at such a time,
And I had set myself to watching, when
A light shone suddenly into my room,
And then I feared a thunderbolt had fired

Some fated vessel on this lonely coast.
So I threw on my cloak and hastened out,
All fearful that my fears were certainties,
And that my eyes should see another wreck.
So now I'm joyful, being undeceived,
Although to find you here, Mark, at this hour,
In this vocation, sadly puzzles me.
Are you not ill?   Your face looks very pale;
Your eyes have not their old accustomed look,
But wear an aspect wild and wandering,
As if some trouble preys upon your mind,
And all your manner seems distracted too."

    One foam-white hand falls gently on the sleeve
Of his rough jacket with a tender grace,
While a young fear looks from those darling eyes
And steals o'er all those lovely lineaments,
Imparting an inquiring earnestness,
Ev'n blending with the music of her voice.
"Do tell me, pray, what means this midnight toil;
Why burns this beacon on this lonely spot?
Oh, what if some poor toiling mariners
Should see its glimmer shining from afar,
And take it for a friendly guide designed
To show their storm-tossed ship a welcome port!

How sad would be such a catastrophe,
When waking from this dream of danger past—
Of needed rest in sweet security,
They look and see but death stands black before !
The very thought of it disturbs my soul,
And makes me feel almost as cold as death.
But, Mark, I'm sure you did not think of that ;
Your generous heart would not have bid the risk.
Come ! tell me all at once, for a strange fear
Is creeping o'er me like an icy chill."

Still the fandango of the gods goes on !

V.

   Still the wild tumult of the night goes on !
But what is that to those that shake the soul—
Those stormful storms within that shake the soul,
And rock the slender tower of their faith
Who know not that behind this discord dark—
This seeming hap-hazard of crazy fate—
Lurks the small germ of an immortal joy,
As life lurks in corruption.   Who know not
That these high thrills of wild and sweet regret
Are prophesies of passion, piercing, pure,
Aspiring to regain her ancient sway
Over her darkened and engulfed domain.

See how these wakeful hearts torment themselves
With vague but sweet and subtle mysteries!
Quite heedless of the outer storm they stand,
Immersed in shifting waves of yellow light
That weave weird wizzards on the warped walls
Standing up old and haggard on the sky,
A growing rent in night's monastic robe,
Which hasty hands in vain attempt to mend,
Her gaze, half-fearful and half-pleading, meets
In his changed orbs a new and sudden light;
His bosom lifts and sinks, his warrior's form
Seems to experience a magic growth;
His strong brown hand has clasped the foam-white one
That fluttered bird-like on his sinewy arm;
His vivid face betrays a rosy flush,
Imparted by no outward circumstance;
His voice has caught a thrill of ecstacy—
The strong sweet music of a lover's tones.
" Come farther in the firelight; these sea winds
Are full of damp diseases; I would hold
Myself a guilty wretch did you take ill
In consequence of this experience.
Now calm, I pray you, your excited fears,
And listen while I briefly answer make;
For, Mora, I have much to say to-night

Which may not bide a more propitious time.
I could not sleep nor rest; my mind, alert,
Required employment, and my hands did yield
Unto its fierce demand and formed this pile
To lend a constant color to the scene.
And this is why I hover like a bird
Of ill portent o'er this old monument.
Upon my soul I did not think of harm
To any wandering creatures of the sea!
My only wish was to combat the fiend
That tortures me so terribly to-night.
Oh, Mora! I have had such wicked dreams
Through all the terrors of this wicked night!
My mind, I think, would have been wholly lost,
Amid the press of swift and tempting shapes,
Had I not thought of you, and so was saved.
Your spirit's presence checked its onward drift,
And caused a calm temper to prevail.
Oh you have power to change at once for aye
This doubting, fearing state—this living death—
For one of constant and substantial joy!
You are the umpire of a fearful game
Between the destinies that play for souls!
Mine's now at stake—with you the issue rests—
With your affection, life and hope and joy!

Without it, doom too hard to contemplate—
A doom whose very shadow shakes the soul!
When first I told you of my passion's birth,
You bade me wait 'till time had rendered you
A better knowledge of a heart too young
To know the nature of its tender need.
So I have waited—waited on for years,
Without another hope to solace me
Save that uncertain one.   No more, no more
Leave me to preying doubts, but let this hour
Become my Delphi, you the oracle,
Proclaiming auguries of weal or woe!
Oh darling! darling! I can love with love
More strong than yonder ocean in his strength,
Constant to thee as to the moon his tides!
All shall be thine—aye, all—I'll worship thee
With all the passion of a tropic heart,
I promise all a woman's heart can crave
Of love and peace and sunshine of the soul—
Realization of the fondest dreams
That ever fired a breast with sweet desires.
Ay, I dare promise everything of worth
If you will place your dear heart in my trust.
Speak quick, and say how it shall be with me!
So, darling, so! now answer from thy heart!"

His arm has drawn her slender form to him,
Her luscious lips have felt his thrilling kiss,
Her lustrous eyes have drunk his thirsting glance,
Her senses almost reel; but she protests,
Struggling, though gently, in his close embrace,
More beautiful in this her maiden shame,
More warmly, sweetly human than before!
O moment of unutterable joy,
To him whose heart is love, and love is heaven!
O bright spot 'twixt two wastes all desolate—
All destitute of any freshening spring
Where a toil-spent and weary soul may quaff
The fresh and renovating cup of life!
One, the bare desert of unfruitful years,
The other—draw the veil, man cannot view
With his weak earthly eyes its mysteries,
And hope to slumber quietly again.
Ah, let us hover closer to these too!
For we were mortal once, and so have felt
These sweet sensations warm the willing blood,
Which in one moment of its tender rage
Holds more of truth than slow and weary fears
Of slavish toil for knowledge can attain.
But listen while the scenic vision winds
On toward the entrance of that higher stage,

Whose flaming lights are in the actors' eyes.
" No, Mark, not so, that was a wicked kiss !
Release me, pray—'tis shame to hold me thus !
Oh what could prompt an act so dangerous !
None ever treated me this way before !
But now be calm and hear what I've to say ;
That I do fully understand you now
I cannot doubt ; poor Mark ! I did not think
That my imprudent words were so construed
As to promote this passion in your breast
Which I regarded as a transient thing,
Born of an idle fancy of the hour.
Would I had known the nature of your heart
Ere you had fed yourself so long on hope !
I long have thought that you had ceased to feel
For me as any but a brother feels
Toward a true and only sister ; so
The tender subject you have broached to-night
Recalls something I had forgotten quite.
Oh ! do not stare me in that awful way !
I do believe you love me as you say,
Though why 'tis so I cannot understand.
I'm but a weak, perhaps a fickle, girl,
Without accomplishments or arts beyond
What nature and my humble station gave ;

Unworthy to possess a love like yours—
Incompetent, I fear, to comprehend
A nature so much subtler than my own,
So high removed from my poor little world.
Hear and believe me, I conjure you, Mark;
Be calm and think, and you'll perceive at once—
Will realize as I do that 'tis best
We should remain as we have ever been
Toward each other, dear and faithful friends;
That natures separated as are ours
By such an intellectual barrier,
In forming this most sacred tie of earth,
Should choose each one a more congenial soul.
Go mingle with the world that you have shunned—
The world that has a balm for every wound—
And find affection that your nature craves,
Where every impulse is interpreted,
And love possesses knowledge to perceive
The soul's distemper and apply the cure.
You have a genius that would win you fame,
And love and honor, in its proper sphere;
Why let it, then, drift on this dubious tide,
Subjected to the world's most killing shocks?
Why not aspire to lead it higher up,
And place it where it may expand and shine,

Secure among its kindred elements?
Mark, my preserver, I have wronged you much
In keeping you in this anxiety ;
Say you forgive me, and I will atone
For past neglect by yielding you that love
Which burns the purer, having less of self—
The gentle reverence of a sister's heart.
Say you forgive me and accept my gift
(Renewed—redoubled—since you love me so),
Thus we may banish all unhappiness ;
For I am sure you have weighed well my words
And clearly see how near they touch the truth.
Then we will quit this evil spot. Come, come."

　　An icy light has crept into his eyes
While drinking in her golden wine of words—
A light so deeply piercing, and intense
In its wild fixedness that all the face
Seems turned to marble in its pallid blaze.
Thrice he essays to speak, and thrice his voice
Fails like the effort of a freezing man.
A moment, and the power comes ebbing back
In chilling ice streams trickling from his lips,
Which yield them passage as it were by force.
" You have not told me all—something remains
Which you in vain are trying to conceal !

Mora, my sight is very clear to-night!
Methinks I see a shadow on your heart—
A human shadow, which absorbs in you
The fresh stream of your thoughts as it runs on
With all its native fire and energy.
Something you hope—something anticipate,
More than your lips have yet disclosed to me.
Perched like a bird upon yon dizzy crag,
To-day I saw you looking out to sea,
Long, with your glass bent on the horizon,
To every point the bold lookout exposed;
Oft you would turn away, as oft *return*,
And gaze as if your soul was in your eyes;
Then with impatient gesture sit you down,
And toss loose pebbles down into the sea,
To which you seemed to be addressing words,
As if endeavoring to work a charm
Upon the idle waters of the main.
The circumstance most unaccountably
Called up a restless spirit on my mind,
Who tortured me with unremitting spite,
Till suddenly he ceased, and whispering said,
In chuckling accents from his husky throat:
'The sea bird looketh for her absent mate,
Who rideth home on hot wings from afar.'

You have a lover on the sea to-night,
Whose welfare is your great solicitude.
I know it! it was not enough to know
That I must crave so fondly and in vain
That joy which is the essence of all joys,
Without the awful fact that I must live
To see it added to another's lot!"

E'en as he speaks the current slowly thaws,
As in the light of a returning sun;
And now the moist proof gems the dusky fringe
That hangs upon the margin of those wells
Of changing passion, deep and wonderful.
"But I am wild and know not what I say!
And though I struggle to be rational,
Love is unreasoning, and will not yield
Her lawless empire to cold logic's sway.
Nay, do not speak—I know what you would say—
That he is noble, generous and brave.
I fully understand your woman's heart,
And trust its longings may be realized—
That heaven may bring him safely to your arms.
Your hand! for I accept your proffered gift,
And pledge myself to keep it sacred as
The struggling soul to which I fold it close.
By a quick flash of reason I perceive

How much of truth your reasoning comprehends,
How deeply wiser woman is than man,
How quicker to dive to the heart of things,
And bring up hidden knowledge to the light.
You have divined the structure of my soul
By an admirable insight, but who
Shall analyze these phantoms of my brain !
This clear cool glance shall flee like airy shape
Before the light of my attendant moon,
Whose mystic rays again traverse my brain.
I hold a desolating genius whose
Strange cravings naught on earth can satisfy,
A gnawing hunger for—I know not what—
Born with my birth and nursed by circumstance,
Outstripping will in a neglected soil—
A garden given to the growth of chance.
It is a primitive and fixed decree,
A burden I must bear unto the end
Without the knowledge of its source or aim.
Oh, will these straightening tortures never cease !
See you yon precipice's awful jaw ?

Hear you those wolves that cry for mortal prey ?
But, Mora, come ; this is no place for you ;
The fire is almost out, the clamorous hour
Suits not the tender nature of your thoughts

Leave me to its familiar fantasies—
Ah, leave me to my madness and the storm!
But what a fool!   Come, Mora, take my arm,
This once, at least, I'll be like other men—
Gods! that's the *soul* of all the elements!"

    A blinding flash that seems to split in twain
Heaven's overcrowded amphitheatre,
Jumps from the folds of an o'erhanging cloud,
Leaps crackling down the staircase of the sky,
And plunges hissing in the boiling brine,
Leaving the darkness to reverberate
With hollow bellowings from the throat of night.
A low cry quivers from the maiden's lips,
She seizes with a quick convulsive hand
Her dark companion's poised outpointing arm,
Points with the other out along the sea—
Along the rising sinking hills of sea—
And cries with terrified distracted voice,
" Look, Mark! oh God! I see it there—a ship!
'Tis gone—it hung all quivering on the top
Of a gigantic overwhelming wave!
I saw it there as plainly as could be!
'Tis as I feared—this light has guided here
Some hapless sailors of the midnight sea!

Oh, Mark! you are a man—do something, pray!
Shout—shriek—and warn them ere it is too late!"

 " Already 'tis too late! the stern decree
Has passed, and here I stand a murderer!
His will be done who aimed this awful blow!
Now, Heaven, let thy unhappy creature die! . . .
My race is up—my being's unknown sun
Goes out and leaves its baser tenement
Low smouldering in the ruin of its fall!
Now yells again that demon in my ears—
'Mad as the storm, in storm thy star shall set!'
Now those dim objects in my horizon
Start from their places, form, and wall me in
A wall that has a thousand burning eyes!
Welcome, thou last and consummating curse
And swallow up the creature of thy love!"
His voice rings shrilly out upon the air,
Piercing the maiden's ear like the last note
Of dying hope unto a waiting soul.
As she attempts to speak, another flash,
As fearful quite as the preceding one,
White sparkling, lights again the awful vault,
Showing a scene to touch the toughest heart,
And wring a wail of pity from the lips
Sealed up for years against compassion's voice.

Hardly a stone's throw from the grim sea wall,
Beset by ocean's maddened, yelling pack
Of thirsting beasts, a solitary bark
With tattered sails far streaming in the gale,
And spars and masts reduced to splintered wrecks,
Comes flying on to meet her certain doom
As if she struggles in destruction's cause.
Around her quivering hull the cloven spray,
Like nest of ghastly hissing serpents writhes,
Enfolding her in monstrous lividness.
Now treading on a shifting mountain's top,
She seems to rend her thick habiliment
And fling a high defiance at her foes;
Now plunged in foamy troughs she disappears,
To stagger blind, bewildered from the bout,
And dash in fury at her enemies.
In vain—each change but brings her nearer on—
On to her stern and steadfast destiny.
Nor is this all the powerful eye commands;
Look to her deck—behold the horror there!
Above the cowering figures of his mates,
Upon the shivered bowsprit's heel is seen
A form almost gigantic in its mould,
With wild fair hair that streams like midnight sun
From a bold face set in the type of death

And pierced with eyes like wells of liquid steel,
Whose look is fastened on the horrid goal—
Fixed and unquailing as two tiger eyes.
With gladiatorial shoulders backward thrown,
One broad palm shadowing the wall-like brow,
The other closed around a straining stay,
He towers grandly up to meet the shock,
Heroic daring in his attitude.
Night's instant curtain closes out the whole.
A terror-telling shriek, pealed from white lips,
Depicts the anguish which the spectacle
Has crowded on the girl's affrighted heart ;
And like a lost wind wailing in the wilds,
The words well from her overburdened breast—
" 'Tis he! 'tis he!—my poor, my poor Eugene !
Gone—lost forever !"   Down her wilting form
Falls, like a lightning-blighted flower to earth,
And at the feet of him who, statue-like,
Stands with one hand pressed to his raining brow,
As if a bolt from heaven had nailed him there,
And chained him to a still eternal dream.

What horror next ?   A cry, a crash, a rush,
Slow struggling up amidst the general roar,
Tell that the wolves have overhauled their prey.
Now dances on the air a maniac laugh,

Sad and unearthly as a panther's cry,
Floating away upon the wing of winds,
And mingling with the voices of the storm,
" Mad as the storm, in storm thy star shall set."
Shall set, ha !—ha ! but shall not set alone !
The bloody wolves are at their meal down there !
I see their white teeth flashing through the gloom,
I hear them roar and wrestle o'er their prey.
Were I a wolf I'd join the banquet too,
A human wolf would win the greater share.
Oh, how these little vermin gnaw my brain,
Tearing its smarting texture into shreds !
Oh heaven ! oh cease ! so, I'll be calm again.
Come, Mora, come and see this glorious wreck.
How still she lies ! come, Mora, darling, come,
And let us find your lover—your Eugene !
I hear him crying out for us to come ;
I see him beckoning from out the waves,
His face as red and round as any moon,
Set in the green side of a glassy sea.
But come ! he'll weary if we linger long."
Snatching her lifeless body from the rock,
With quick strong bounds he gains the giant's brow,
Holding his burden lightly on his arm,
As if it were no more than feather's weight.

Pausing, he presses on her passive lips,
Grown wondrous cold since last he tasted them,
A hundred kisses, burning and intense,
Like hot wine poured between a statute's lips—
Lips that change not their cold disdainful curl,
Or yield a sign responsive to the glow,
And laugh and sparkle of the lordly draught.
A stream of lightning trickles down the sky,
Showing the face he heaps his kisses on
Set like a picture in its ebon frame—
Its ebon frame of coiling clinging hair.
A flash of reason piercing through the dense
Confusèd mass of his entangled brain,
Conveys the truth with overwhelming force.
A wailing cry comes up out of the rush
Of jostling demons—then "There streams his hair,
Like the red ghost light of a spectre ship !
See where he points his white and dripping hands,
And motions us to follow him—come, come ! "

"Come, come ! " the tempest's trumpeters repeat,
And the wild revel of the night roars on !

VI.

A splendid morn ! by Jove, a lovely morn !
See burning Sol rise from his ocean bath,

Genial and ruddy with his early sport—
Smiling and panting with his lusty sport.
See how he pauses with a god-like grace
To kiss the dim tears from sweet nature's face.
Now with his flaming circlet on his brow,
And airy step, he mounts his golden car
To lead the gliding train of happy hours
Along the breezy avenues of heaven,
Accompanied by mingled minstrelsy
Of mellow harps strung to delightful airs.
Mark how the glad waves laugh with rich delight,
And show their white teeth in their soft conceit—
Flash their white teeth beneath the lifting folds
Of gauzy drapery mantling their fresh couch;
Breathing soft gossip to the tell-tale wind,
Who flies with it o'er isles and continents
Reposing in the scented lap of morn.
The restless sea birds, with diffusive joy,
Throng on the scene from wide dissevered homes;
To drink the red wine from morn's gracious hand;
To drink till cries attest their high delight;
Drink drunk and reel and wet their gay attire,
Then with amusing rage turn on the sea
And plunge their beaks into his happy breast,
Which heaves and trembles with a hearty glee—

Shakes with strong mirth at their discomfiture.
As seaside beauties tempt the playful waves
With heavenly glimpses of delicious limbs,
'Till grown o'erdaring in their sportiveness,
They laugh and leap and grow competitors
In feats of pretty waywardness, when up,
Out of deceiving quiet, suddenly,
Leaps with loud rush a pack of lusty waves,
And throw themselves among the startled nymphs—
Right in among them, wetting them all o'er,
And causing many pretty shrieks of fright
As they break in a bevy up the bank.
So do these foolish gulls amuse themselves
With screams and clamor at each slight mishap.

But what are these from which the waves recoil,
Pressing back on their fellows suddenly,
As if they fear to tread the shining sands
Which bear their foot-prints of unnumbered years?
What are those forms reposing on the beach,
Silent among the fragments of a wreck,
Piled up by ocean in his angry mood?
Have they no welcome for the happy guest
Who comes with smiles to touch their lazy limbs,
To drop warm kisses on their drowsy lids?
Come, let us hover through their morning dreams,

And pull the sleepy tyrant from his throne.
Why does this beauteous mortal slumber here,
With tangled seaweed twisted in her hair—
The crown of Neptune on her lovely head,
As if she waits upon her bridal couch
Till dawns the hour that brings her absent groom?
The gray old god has won her with his wiles,
Has charmed her sweet soul from its tenement,
Which now lies beautiful but desolate.
Yes, Ocean, smitten with her fairy grace,
Has led her through the maze of mystic forms
Inhabiting his city's wide suburbs,
Down to the gorgeous chambers of his court
Adorned with splendid spoils from countless wrecks,
Wove in and blended with delightful skill
With all the royal riches of his realm;
Where joy's voluptuous wing untiring fans
The melting flame of unrestricted love;
And time is lost in music, song and dance,
And passion's hot and sweet bewilderment,
Where she shall reign sea queen—but what is here?
A Saxon giant, with his Saxon hair
Trailed like a conquered banner on the sands;
His wrestler's form—his tempest-tempered bulk,
In all the seeming vigor of its youth—

Its perfect natural manhood, strength and pride,
Stretched stiff and passive, with its lamp gone out;
The cold film gathered o'er those azure globes
Which rolled the light of heaven upon his brain,
Ere ocean dashed his bold hand over them
And fixed them in their marble sullenness.
And this is what it is to be a man
Of massy mould, opposing time and change,
Vain of superior perishable strength!
Ah! was he more in ocean's choking grasp
Than you frail angel form reposing there?
His stout impetuous heart presumed too much,
And the old god, who brooks no rivalry,
Rose up and crushed him to his mother's feet!

But here behold the glory of the world—
The earthy vessel of celestial wine,
Cracked—shattered on the border rocks of life;
The herald of imperishable truth,
A poet-hero of the darling race
Of gods, the light and wonder of the world,
A lifeless burden on his mother earth,
As if his were no more than common clay.
Heaven-sent with tidings from the Infinite;
Full of the wild sublimity of things,
The sweet and touching tenderness of things;

With power to utter in a few swift words
Truths high and shining as the solar soul;
To string upon a thread of thrilling notes
Gems plucked from the Eternal's awful throne,
To waken and reanimate the world—
Behold the champion of his troubled race
Reft of his vivifying prophet fire;
Forlorn, neglected, dead, as exiles die—
As He, yea, He, the poet-god of woe—
E'en He, the Prince of Peace and sorrowing song,
Fell when fierce folly in his desperate mood,
Struck the life-lamp from truth's all-healing hand!
O blind old world! so blundering obstinate!
When will you cease to stumble blindly on
Through the thick gulf of old obscurity,
Nor heed the songs thy trembling singers sing,
Of love, and peace and worshipful repose?
When will you strive to make more smooth their ways,
Who pour their generous wine into thy wounds,
And humor you when you are sick and sad?
How long must angels see such sights as these?
Is this a fit fate for a son of song?
Beware, you who are lukewarm in their cause—
Who from indifference permit such things—
Such damning rot-proofs to accumulate!

The eye is on you, terrible and bright—
The eye that never sleeps for watchfulness
Over God's woeful wandering messengers.
See this poor fallen hero where he lies,
His thrilling harp strings snapped by lawless death.
Where are the hands that should have led him on
O'er the rough path with tender care,
And kept him from heart-biting bitterness ?
There'll be a new star in the heavens to-night,
While earth shall flounder on through seas of gloom ;
While men will hug their golden falsehoods close,
Unmindful of the hope that's dead to them !
But let us lift our vision from this scene.
Oh let us fly this piteous sight !   Come, come !

And the grand chariot of day rolled on.

DRIFT FROM A WRECK

POETA MARINA.

ROLLED and tumbled and tossed about,
  Like a beaten wreck by the reckless sea,
All over and under and in and out
  And among the waters that compass me.
Now lifted high up by the waterspout,
  Then plunged down low as a man may be.

Thrown from my shore in a moonland trance,
  And bound to the back of an uncouth beast,
That plunges round in a drunken dance,
  Like a chip thrown in midst the breakers' yeast,
I am gazing out over the years for a glance
  Of my cliff's dim rising against the east.

The boatswain that whistles the winds to play,
  And the waves to dance with destructive leap,
Has seen me through many a weary day
  Hung on the verge of the watery steep,
With a calm eye bent down the rugged way,
  And a hand to the wheel with a steady sweep.

A man of strange wanderings and woes,
 With a brain locked fast on an antique dream,
I bid adieu to my friends and foes,
 I kiss my hand to my hill and stream,
And turn and go down where the salt breeze blows,
 And the torn foam-banners career and gleam.

I strip myself of my robes of pride,
 And brace my limbs for the terrible fight;
I thrust the trembling fears aside,
 And set my course by the sea bird's flight,
To follow where boreal tempests ride
 O'er islands drowned in the wild north light.

Sometimes through desolate seas I plough
 With never a zephyr to fill my sail,
With never a billow to lift my prow
 Or a spirit to breathe me a moving tale,
And a gaunt bird hovering o'er my bow,
 With a form like death and a face as pale.

Oft on the horizon a sail will rise,
 And beckon to me like a spirit hand
Waved from a casement in painted skies,
 To bid me stay on some sunshine strand;
And some of them pass from my aching eyes,
 To rise no more upon any land.

With a firm faith fixed on the true and strong,
    And a hard grim grip on the things that be,
I look aloft as I heave along,
    Drinking the light with heroic glee,
Planting the germs of a deathless song
    Deep down where never an eye can see.

Tumbled about in a desperate way,
    Hither and thither and everywhere;
Grasping such pleasure as comes to stay,
    Fighting the demons of old despair
With a brave heart set for the port of day,
    And a hope as strong as the strong light there.

Singing, God in his wisdom afflicteth me,
    And therefore I'll make it a joy to bear;
From a world as full as a world can be
    Of every trouble and grief and care,
With a moonland strength I will shake me free,
    When my cliffs ride by in the murky air.

A RELIC.

WITHERED limb of a plant that has perished,
  Some symbolical oak of the past,
Which the race in its infancy cherished
  Ere it bowed to the boreal blast.

Some old tree in whose boughs the first singers
  Of the earth oped their wonderful throats,
To those songs whose quaint melody lingers
  Even yet in a few scattered notes.

Torn away from a trunk in the ages
  When the world and its garments were new,
I was blown through time's various stages,
  By a storm that incessantly blew.

By a tempest that bloweth forever,
  Wafted down through the hurrying years,
'Till I stand by life's full brimming river,
  In amazement and terror and tears.

Mournful type of a nation forgotten
  Ere the tresses of time had grown gray,
I have slept till the old world is rotten,
  And awake to its stain and decay.

Out of time, out of place and mistaken,
  Long I've sought and in vain for a soul—
For a heart and a spirit unshaken
  By these waters that ceaselessly roll.

By these billows so restlessly rolling
  On the sea-eaten walls of the world,
With an echo like fog alarms tolling
  Where the wings of the mist are unfurled.

Yes, I've sought till my feet are aweary,
  And my brave heart as heavy as lead—
Oh how fearfully lonesome and dreary
  Is the path an unloved one must tread.

Men are born and men die, still I tarry
  In this cold habitation of men,
And await the slow tide that shall carry
  This old hulk to its harbor again.

As a vine that is sorrowfully clinging
  To some hoary old ruin of yore,
Or a bird in the wide desert singing
  Melodies of a long lost before.

THE DAYS TO COME.

O MOURNFUL melancholy years gone by,
  Ye are but ghosts! but ah, the ones to come!
  I think of what they promise and am dumb;
I dream of them and waken with a cry
Wrung from the depths of some great agony,
  Too wild and deep for language to become.

Let others mourn for years that are no more,
  I'll weep for weary days that are to be,
  Ere I shall touch that far soil of the free
Where my free soul roamed in some glorious yore,
For some immortal sin cast to this shore
  Pursued by dim unhappy memory.

IN QUARANTINE.

IN quarantine, with a scorching sky,
  A sultry air and a glassy sea,
On which the masts' tall shadows lie,
  And the sea-bird drifts in a reverie;
Day after day on the dreamy eye
  The changeless scene weighs dreamily!

All motionless the black hulks sleep,
 Like torpid monsters in the sun,
Save when they swing with the lazy sweep
 Of the languid tides as they idly run
Through days and weeks that slowly creep
 Toward a goal that is never won.

Low on our lee the emerald keys
 Like sentries, guard the northern pass,
And the listless eye of the gazer sees
 Their forms as through a shadowed glass,
And where their chain sinks in the seas,
 The reef light's gray gigantic mass.

Scattered along the enameled coves
 The city's gleaming structures stand,
Looking seaward from cocoa groves
 Like a happy vision of fairy-land,
Or as some scenic picture moves
 O'er a stage strewn over with golden sand.

Yon gray old sailor who ruminates
 O'er his navy plug with an idle air,
Directs the gaze of his lolling mates
 To the high martello's massive square,
As with a shudder he demonstrates
 How "the devil has hoisted his pennant there."

Then well these grim tars understand
  That the yellow admiral's on a cruise,
And they tell with a tragic mein and grand
  Wild stories of ships and their ghostly crews,
Drifting leagues and leagues from any land,
  While death was the dearest mate to choose.

At morn the drowsy sentry sees,
  With a pang he struggles to suppress,
A mournful group among the orange trees,
  Gathered in prayerful and fixed address,
And mutters, affecting a yawn of ease,
  "They're planting another 'case,' I guess."

Ay, Jack, your terrible namesake's here,
  With badge and banner wide displayed,
Charging the lurid atmosphere
  With the poison of the everglade;
If your Uncle Sam don't interfere
  He's likely to drive you a lively trade.

In quarantine—ah, for a chase
  With the dancing waves of the open main!
Oh, for a briny breeze to brace
  The slumbering energies again,
And spur our winged steed to the race
  With the riders of the hurricane!

THE ADMIRAL.

He walks the deck with firm elastic step,
And speaks his few commands in kindly tones,
Which have not lost their music since the time
That heard them thrilling through the deafening din
And rush and thunder of the battle rout—
That strong inspiring quality of voice
Sounding long after in the hearers' ears,
Like echoes of a half-remembered dream.

A gray and grand old man, whose sturdy frame
Bears yet no trace of physical decay,
Despite the shocks it has experienced—
The battle blows and tempests of its time—
One of those rare and pleasing spectacles
Of unimpaired vitality in age,
Which reconcile us to the thought that rise
With mournful languor from the great to-be.
So like the mighty heroes of old time,
The mighty men of Britain and of Rome,
And th' iron founders of our liberties,
Whose grateful pictures, stamped upon our hearts
Among the deep impressions of our youth,
Afford us rapture in maturer years,
And give a tone and color to our lives.

With general manner courteous and kind,
Too genial-hearted for formality;
A sailor's disregard of any rule
In free discourse—a happy medium
Unconsciously correct; a generous warmth,
And equal flow of human sentiment,
Enriched by sparkles of spontaneous wit,
With lumps of humor now and then thrown in—
A trait that wins all guests unwittingly,
Delighting all who come within its scope
Like circulating draughts of rare old wine,
He stands a noble chieftain every inch,
And every inch a man. A steady eye,
Blue as the bluest sea he sails upon,
Clear with the light of a courageous soul—
That courage which flashed out so brilliantly
Amid the dreadful ruin and the wreck
That strewed the gun-stunned waves of Mobile Bay;
The fiery spirit of resistance which
Flamed up so fiercelessly on that dreadful day,
That when the shell directed at his heart
Saw there a rage so grander than its own—
A fire and force eclipsing its desire,
A soul of valor burning like the sun,
It turned aside and smote the hero's arm—

Struck off the stout left arm stretched out to hurl
His host of ocean tigers on the foe.

Methinks I see him in his glory's hour,
As *they* beheld him, stationed at his post;
Directing in his stern defiant mood
His concentrated thunder on the lines
Of hostile batteries blazing red with death;
Behold him ere the battle shade has yet
Passed from his eyes, or from his Vulcan form
The high heroic grandeur has relapsed;
While at his feet along the riven deck
A strange red wine stands round in little pools,
Which men lie down beside as if to drink,
But seized with sudden full forgetfulness
While in the act, lie there so rapt—so still—
Quite as oblivious of the row around,
As if they slept in pleasant fields afar,
With soft winds sighing through their summer dreams.

Yes; oft in dreams I see it pictured forth
In all its dread details; a drifting cloud,
With panoramic pictures woven in,
Illumined and made vivid by a form
Of luminous distinctness in the midst—
A vision that breaks in upon the night

Of darkest thoughts, and drowns their shadows back
O'er the dead walls of the material world,
They rise behind with dull and frightful stare;
A light that floods with sudden radiance
The airy chambers and majestic halls
Of the mind's ornamented palaces,
Revealing each god in his lofty niche,
Each marble warrior on his pedestal,
And all the rich and glorious spoils that years
Have added to adorn the sacred place;
Spoils wrung from horny-handed circumstance,
Or dug from mouldering ruins of the past :—
A flash—a thrill of joyful ecstacy,
That sends a rich warm rush of golden words,
Like liquid sunshine, bubbling to the lips;
A stream of song that struggles to be free,
And writhes and wrestles like a conscious thing
To sing of him who is a singer too—
A singer, too, of wild unwritten songs–
Of sweet heart-songs that lead him to the shrine
Of love, where he, a constant votary,
Receives the heart's unerring prophecies.
Hail! hail! my hero! from my ocean scenes
I shout to you amid the hurricane—
The clash and clamor of the elements;

Climb to the summit of my shifting hills
To catch the ribboned splendor of your star
Set in the ragged fringes of the storm;
To take its winy light beneath my cloak,
And bear it like a lamp along with me
Down to my twilight regions, there to sit
Within its light and weave my old sea dreams.

SOLVED.

How is it that whichever way I turn,
  Be it upon the land or on the sea,
Where ice-cliffs glitter or sun-splendors burn,
  Some thing in nature has a song for me—
  A measured greeting voiced in melody;
Sad, sweet, sometimes, as wailings of a soul
  Lost in the wilds of an immortal grief;
Sometimes sublime as wild hurrahs that roll
  A savage welcome to a savage chief;
  Calm, tempered, often, as a saint's belief?

How is it that amidst decay or bloom
  Some thing of low or eminent degree
Holds the ripe word, which spoken at the tomb
  Of mouldering remembrance closed to me,
  Sets all their long-forgotten phantoms free;

Free thence to wander many a night and day
  Through the well kept apartments of my brain,
And bathe with fresh delight in the clear ray
  Of living sunshine pouring through each pane,
  Strange to my thoughts, but welcome in their train?

Not always is the wished-for music heard,
  Nor can it come by bidding of the will;
But in rare moments when the heart is stirred
  With nameless strange disquiet at some ill
  At which the wild soul flies with daring skill;
Or after aching toil or thought intense,
  When o'erwrought nature strives in sleepless throes,
It comes, a balm, to soothe the straining sense—
  To lull the irritated nerves, and close
  A gate of gold between me and my woes.

Not through medium of the carnal ear,
  Stunned by earth's clamors, is the sound conveyed;
But by some fine internal sense more near
  The sacred citadel where stands arrayed
  Love, faithful sentinel, and undismayed;
Too coarse, indeed, the senses to detect
  Those immaterial messengers who use
That inarticulate pure dialect
  Which spirit speaks to spirit, and the muse
  Assimilates and struggles to diffuse.

In places desolate and ways obscure,
   In wide lands wasted by the curse of God,
In judgment righteous of stain impure,
   Their voices greet me from the blistered sod,
   Mourning the weight of the avenging rod;
So touching and so plaintive—so instinct
   With penitential sorrow is the song,
Addressed to me as to a being linked
   To them by bond of sacred friendship strong,
   My heart bows down beneath their burden long.

From ruins of old architectural pride,
   And heathen grandeur smitten with decay,
Where pitying ivy spreads her veil to hide
   Their naked ugliness from Christian day,
   Their tones salute me like a trumpet's bray;
Warlike, inspiring, glorious in their strength,
   They wake an antique spirit in my breast—
Some smouldering old heroic fire at length
   Roused from the ashes where it lay repressed,
   Biding its time, a still undreamed-of guest.

In mystic moon-drowned landscapes brooded o'er
   By the chaotic soul of silence throned
Invisibly on night's mysterious shore,
   Commanding voices call me, spirit-toned,
   In purer tongue than mortal ever owned;

But now a strain of soul-fed eloquence,
    At which some kindred genius starts awake
Within my breast, spurning the heathen sense,
    Recalling a lost state where tongue but spake
    Th' eternal truths of which the pure partake.

They call to me from out the hearts of trees,
    They speak to me among the throngs of men;
I hear their voices in the surge of seas,
    I catch their whispers in the stony glen,
    And in the mazes of the treacherous fen;
O sacred sweet companionship! to me,
    Foredoomed to speak th' inevitable thing
That cuts me off from human sympathy,
    What recompense for hate's base serpent-sting,
    To draw my draught from life's perennial spring!

They say my veins are fresh—that I am young
    In face and fancy—yet I'm very old;
Was old, perhaps, when earth from chaos sprung
    And souls were clothed in suits of sensate mould,
    Ere death was known, or sin, or thirst for gold;
Or the cold sinking fear that pierces deep
    Down to the quick, like thrust of bayonet,
Nameless and formless hanging on our sleep,
    The angel that forbids us to forget,
    Lest drunk with hope we cease to feel our debt.

Yes, I am old; so old, I do believe,
  That when on certain forms and scenes I bend,
After the first faint flash I can perceive
  The subtle presence of an ancient friend,
  A recognition which I somehow blend—
Blend with a memory stretching back and back,
  Across the buried ages, to a shore
Beyond the utmost of time's lengthy track,
  Where hand in hand in some all-glorious yore,
  We, free, pure souls, went seeking golden lore.

O bright etherial spirits once so free,
  With whom I wandered in that region wide,
Now 'neath the rugged rinds of plant and tree,
  And in rude cells of earth doomed to abide
  Till into horrible decay they slide;
They are *your* voices that I recognize,
  In varied tones of gladness raised to greet
Their old and loved companion of the skies
  Who stumbles over earth with heavy feet,
  Mewed like an eagle in his frail retreat.

GLIMPSES.

It was not a mere fantasy of brain,
  That myth of old Pythagoras, who thought
His life the echo of a grander strain,
  Who deemed him blest by recollections brought
  From some far sphere in which his soul had wrought;
No idle tale indeed; for who is there
  That has not viewed sometime in.his career
A scene which memory linked with one somewhere
  Outside the circle of his present sphere,
  Beyond th' abyss of many a mouldered year?

Who has not had those aged memories,
  Unlike th' unstable currency of dreams,
Or fancy's vague irrationalities,
  Dawn full upon him in the midday beams,
  While the fierce blood sang on in blinding streams;
And then the sudden check—the start, as o'er
  Th' arrested senses sped that clear cold wave,
Wafted from seas the soul had sailed before,
  Big with reflections of the great and brave—
  Then passed, and left all deathly as the grave?

Oft as I walk among the mingled throng,
  With thoughts to some absorbing life-theme laced,
A sudden change will fall my frame along—
  A penetrating chill, as if embraced
  By unseen arms in icy mail encased;
I start, perhaps to catch some passer-by—
  Some utter stranger to my mortal sight,
Observing me with an inquiring eye,
  As if he questioned whether it were right
  To hail me comrade in some lost delight.

The bars are burst! then like a swollen lake,
  That tears a channel through the weakened wall,
Strong floods of vivid recollections break
  From some great deep unbroken since the fall,
  And sweep my present thought beyond recall;
There, through the shining spray of rare surprise,
  Mixed in a brief scene of unsinful mirth,
Warmed by sweet light of vanished paradise,
  That face which baffled the dull eyes of earth
  Glows recognized in sight of earlier birth.

A throb—'tis gone—'tis past; and ah, too brief
  The light that linked me with immortal bliss!
Vanished the glimpse of that lost world! in grief
  And half-despair I turn again to this,
  Now marred forever by the serpent's hiss;

A humbled man I pass upon my way,
  Conscious I bear a burden of the crime
That lost mankind a heritage for aye,
  And bound him to this double wheel of time,
  Which grinds his dirge in life's unchanging rhyme.

DRIFTING.

DRIFT, did you say? What can we do but drift—
  Drift with the tide we cannot stem or stay?
  See those who struggle whirled as fast away
As they that calmly watch life-phantoms lift,
Swung to and fro as fates and fortunes shift
  Their feeble lights before the broad bright day.

Those systems surging through eternal space,
  Which hold the secrets of our destiny
  Locked in their circles where no eye can see,
Can they move one jot from their given place—
The path He has marked out for them to trace?
  Then how much less may such dim orbs as we!

A million lives are drifting on to-day
  Among the dubious currents of the time,
  Whose hearts are anchored on the vast sublime,

Nor heed the feeble straws thrown in their way,
The wretched fragments of a world's decay
   The tides wash up from out its settled slime.

Lives that seem to the carnal eye possessed,
   Of every true essential making life
   A joyous feast shut in from noise and strife,
The calm capacities of the earth-blest,
But they are strange wise birds whose lofty nest
   Is earth-remote and safe when storms are rife.

Ay, drift! the shore lies yonder on our lee,
   Its structures brightly lined against the sky,
   So luminous they dim the eager eye
That strains to pierce their mystic drapery;
There, in the end, through storm or calm shall we
   Each clasp the idol sought so earnestly.

For not in vain this one long dream of years—
   This wistful fond imagination bent
   On the ideal with such close intent;
This angel wild with woe and clad in tears
Who pleads our sorrows in celestial ears,
   With strength of woe so daring-eloquent.

No, not in vain; for in the dreamer's mind
  Lie hid the germs of every mighty good ;
  The poet, brooding in his solitude,
Intensely o'er some deep wrong to his kind,
Grasps finally a power undivined
  By all philosophy's wise brotherhood.

A noble work of genius is a prayer—
  A reverent reaching for the Infinite ;
  The peerless painting ravishing the sight,
The massy temple dark'ning in the air,
The songs of bards arising everywhere
  And undefined aspirings to the light.

Think not they are unheard—unheeded all,
  Those earnest cries eluding mortal ear ;
  For these are they which angels stoop to hear—
Ay, one of such unknowingly can call
More heavenly lustre to this earthly ball
  Than wisdom sheds through many a thousand year.

Since men's best deeds are done unconsciously,
  Why be forever caring ? why, indeed,
  Not be like to the poet, taking heed
Of neither time nor fate, but nobly free,
Leave all the rest to God and destiny,
  Loving mankind but craving not their meed.

THE MODERN MARINER.

I.

It was a touching tale he told,
That skinny shell-back gray and old—
  That ancient weather-beaten whale
  Blown to my side by careless gale,
Whose faithful picture is impressed
Upon the life-log of my breast,
  And has a never-failing power
  To soothe me in my ugly hour.

I'll tell it as 'twas told to me
When I was young and fierce and free,
  New wedded to the ocean blue,
  The only bride I ever knew;
Though that was many years ago
I keep it still, I loved it so;
  As told to me, I'll tell it you,
  And reck not whether false or true,
  I argue not—I never do;
I know it left upon my heart
An imprint that will not depart;
  True I believed it then to be,
  So it is true—at least to me;

At all events it well will do
To while an idle hour or two,
   And will, perhaps, some pleasure give
   When I shall have forgot to live.

If sailors, more than other men,
Tell monstrous whoppers now and then,
   It does not follow as a fact,
   That they are liars by the act;
For there's a license granted those
Who lighten thus our cares and woes.
   If strange and wild the tales they tell
   'Tis that their lives are wild as well;
A clever fiction learned in youth
Is oft more prof'table than truth ;
   Besides, 'tis known that sailors' lies
   Are moral lessons in disguise.

He sat beside his polished gun
That grimly slumbered in the sun,
   Hung like a fire-ball in the west
   Above the blue Caribbean's breast;
To hear his yarn we gathered near,
With a common heart and a common ear,
   A rugged but attentive throng
   Of sailor lads, sea-tanned and strong;

And I, with fresh heart opened wide,
The awful moment did abide
 When he would ope his lips to pour
 Some thrilling tale of love or war.
He held in one huge horny hand,
Whereon shone one great golden band,
 A pipe of monstrous calibre,
 His close companion on the sea ;
And in his left he held a pot
From which he drank his Rio hot.
 You would have felt surprise and fear
 To see it steaming disappear,
Then smiled and questioned in your mind
" Are men-of-wars'-men copper-lined ? "
 But he was old and cold of blood,
 From battling time and fate and flood,
Though in his wasted form was seen
A trace of what he once had been—
 Erect and stately as the mast
 Whose shadow on the deck was cast ;
His hair was long and thin and gray,
And o'er his temples all astray ;
 His white and patriarchal beard
 Gave him an aspect sage and weird ;

His cheeks were sunken, but his eye
Shone with heroic brilliancy,
   Which told of manly actions past,
   And courage shining to the last;
His voice was steady, full and strong,
And stirring as a trumpet song,
As he arose and thus addressed the throng.

II.

" 'Twas on the far-off Indian seas
One day, deserted by the breeze,
   We lay slow rocking to and fro
   Beneath the hot sun's waning glow;
The waves around us lay unrolled
In undulating blue and gold,
   With pearls and sapphires here and there
   Sown in the ocean's yellow hair;
While all above, the atmosphere
Was full of sea-dust far and near—
   The bright sirocco dust brought there
   By secret currents of the air,
And sifted down in golden rain
Upon the hot and helpless main.

  " She was as fine a brigantine
  As ever clove the waters green;

A graceful outline, staunchly built,
Hull painted black with band of gilt,
  A mermaid figure-head so true
  It seemed alive when tempests blew—
A topman told me, looking pale,
He'd heard it laughing in a gale.
  Aloft, alow, from bowsprit aft
  She shone the model of a craft,
And every tar swore 'blast his eyes'
She was a princess everywise!
  'Twas glorious to see her reel
  The dizzy miles from off her keel,
A splendid sight to watch her shake
The frightened leagues along her wake,
  And roll them in a mass behind
  As she shot on before the wind!

" The burning day was almost done
And I stood looking at the sun,
  Slow sailing to his port of rest
  In some far harbor of the west—
I, with my darling Eveline,
The dearest girl that e'er was seen.
  She, with one hand upon my arm,
  Stood bound by some mysterious charm—

Some gem of wondrous brilliancy
Wove in the garments of the sea,
　Or beautiful barbaric fire
　Her maiden fancy did admire.
She seemed a matchless work of art,
So motionless in every part—
　A maiden made of tinted stone,
　So still her lustrous beauty shone.
The perfumed breath seemed scarce to move
Between her parted lips of love;
　Around her snowy neck hung curled
　The brightest hair in all the world,
Like golden snares the gold sun weaves
In autumn on the forest leaves;
　Her eyes by some mysterious law
　Were polished mirrors, where I saw
　Myself without a fault or flaw;
Her face was innocence and mirth—
The sweetest face in all the earth.
　All which I loved, but loved her best
　For the pure sunshine of her breast,
Her winsome truthfulness of heart,
And sweet affections free from art.

" She was the aged captain's child,
And all his tedious hours beguiled;

At sea, in port, or quarantine
She ever at his side was seen,
And never wandered thence at all
To flirt or coquet at a ball,
　　Though she possessed that pliant grace
　　Which warms and wins in every place.
She laughed and flung the witty word,
And sang as sweet as any bird,
　　Told tales of lover's hopes and fears
　　That thrilled to joy or moved to tears,
And if a maid e'er loved the sea,
That maiden, I am sure, was she.
　　Rough sailors prayed for her at night
　　Though shy and bashful in her sight,
And blessed her for the grief she felt
When fate with any harshly dealt,
　　And blessed her for the smile she sent
　　When all was happy and content;
Her manner, innocent and free,
Won every heart's true loyalty;
　　The very mention of her name
　　Made every coarse thought flee in shame,
But what was sweeter—more divine,
Her heart, with all its worth, was mine.

" I never knew what I possessed
To win the love of such a breast,
   For I was rough and tough and bold,
   And free and careless of my gold;
Loved the rude tempest and the fight,
And hailed adventure with delight;
   Admired the hardy, manly deed
   Performed in sport or hour of need;
And scorned as much as any can
All signs of weakness in a man;
   But turned with tenderness and care,
   Toward the dear defenceless fair.
If youth's hot blood would oft beguile,
I hated roguery all the while,
And shunned the vices of the vile.
   Perhaps 'twas that I loved her more
   Than any she had met before,
For I did love the darling one
With all the fervor of the sun,
   Nor ever sought it to conceal,
   But told her all with ready zeal,
And she returned my confidence
With mingled modesty and sense.
   I do not know, but it may be

It was for this she clung to me
　With such a fond fidelity—
I'm sure I cared not then to know,
It was enough she loved me so.

　" The red sun melted in the wave
　　And left a halo round his grave—
The life blood of another day
Slain in time's terrible affray;
　The wrinkled face of ocean took
　　At once a worn and troubled look;
His lips seemed opening with a sigh
And murmuring a deep good-bye,
　　Then wrapped in folds of mantling night
　　He seemed to shrink and sink from sight
But the old villain, full of guile,
Was planning mischief all the while !

　" 'Ungracious god ! he's gone,' said she,
And turned her laughing eyes on me,
　' Red-faced and with an angry look
　The fainting world he has forsook,
And left us here without a breeze
To blow us from these idle seas,
　That we might follow in his track
　And coax his better humor back.

No doubt in his gay court above
Some goddess has repelled his love;
  Or in a contest with a peer
  Has felt his adversary's spear,
So, having quarrelled with his fair,
And being out of favor there,
  Thinks doubtless to appease the sting
  With outishness to everything.'

" Charmed with her rosy fancy, I
Sought instantly some apt reply,
  And having caught it, turned to speak,
  When something struck my starboard cheek,
A little puff of wind—a breath—
Yet chilling as the touch of death;
  A blow without a sting or smart—
  And yet it reached my very heart!
I felt my limbs grow sudden weak,
I felt the warm blood fly my cheek,
  And turned my startled eye away
  Lest she should note its altered ray;
I did not think—did not divine,
That *she* could read that quiet sign,
  Did not suppose a child like her
  Could understand that messenger—

Precursor of the hurricane,
That wingèd monster of the main,
  That dreadful enemy of all
  Who climb the south seas' slippery wall;
But she had felt the dread caress
Upon her cheek, and in distress,
  Turned with a look upon her face
  That haunts me yet in many a place,
And saw the fear that filled her heart
Was in my own in counterpart.

  A moment in each other's eyes
  We gazed in trouble and surmise,
And then she spoke in whispered tone,
That sounded all unlike her own,
  'Nay, do not turn your eyes away,
  For fear your trouble to betray!
The warning spirit did not pass
Without his cold salute; alas!
  His touch has left me chill and weak,
  I cannot think, and scarce can speak,
As if that touch had stayed in me
The tide of life that ran so free.
  But there's no time save to prepare
  To meet the fiend that broods the air!

Be brave and pass the warning call,
And I will pray to God for all.
 You made he strong—me only fair,
 Brave men for toil, weak girls for prayer.

" One long fond look, one long deep sigh
That spoke a love in agony—
 A depth of trust and tenderness
 No heart can sound or head can guess—
Affection stronger than our hold
Upon the world a hundred fold.
 And then she slowly turned to go,
 And leave me tugging with my woe ;
But that one fond look fired my soul
With yearning I could not control,
 An energy of love—a fire—
 A heathen spirit's strong desire,
 Yet pure as raptures of the lyre.
I spoke no word, but one loud cry
Tore from my lips in agony,
 My hearts' whole love rushed to my brain,
 And made me reckless and insane ;
I sprang and caught her to my breast
And on her lips fierce kisses pressed—
 Such kisses as immortals drink
 When in the last embrace they sink,

Her cheeks to mine, her lips to mine—
My God! my God! it was divine!
  And were I doomed a hundred years
  To sail through boundless seas of tears,
Without another hope for me
Than that soul-lasting memory,
  That very memory alone
  Would for my every ill atone.

" But while I feasted on her charms
She blushed and struggled in my arms,
  And when at last I let her free
  She turned with lightning eyes on me,
  Her bosom heaving like a sea,
  Cheeks hot and cold alternately,
And looked, in her indignant mien,
The wrathful presence of a queen.
  But almost instantly her face
  Lost of its anger every trace,
And in its place a tenderness
Came, blended with a dear distress,
  As if her heart had power to read
  The fondness that had urged the deed,
Had depth to understand the rage
Of passion bursting from its cage,

While pardoning the daring freak
  That shamed her heart and blushed her cheek;
So, smiling at my abject air,
She left me with the shadows there.

III.

" I shall not linger o'er the things—
The perils and the buffetings
  That followed close upon the rear
  Of that low warning note of fear,
And weary patience with a part
The most of you have got by heart—
  Not from the lips of any man,
  But as true sailors only can;
No need now to enumerate
All the events of that dark date,
  A few facts will suffice to show
  How we received and bore the blow;
How, in the middle of the night,
The fiend came down with all his might,
  And found us all prepared as far
  As lay in human power and prayer;
How, in the first rush of the gale,
We tore the ocean's streaming veil;
  How, to the tempest's frenzied song,
  We danced the shrieking seas along,

Now walled above and all around—
A prisoner in sea-dungeons bound,
　　Then shot into a moving hell
　　Of glassy wave that foamed and fell,
Then seized and pitched aloft so high
The slim masts seemed to rake the sky,
　　While red blades circled everywhere
　　As fiend encountered fiend in air,
And black bombs tumbled to and fro
And burst and shook the deep below—
　　The crazy scare was as a lair
　　Of wild beasts goaded to despair,
That fiercely fought and grimly growled,
And flashed their lightning eyes and howled;
　　Still we, though toys in hands like these,
　　Stood firm and battled with the seas,
Fought hand to hand with steady nerve,
The enemy, nor deigned to swerve,
　　Fought as men fight with mortal foes
　　When multitudes the few enclose,
Till one fierce monster, black as sin,
Stove all our starboard bulwarks in,
　　And pouring on us with his horde
　　Swept half our brave crew overboard,

And others, rushing through the breach,
Swept everything within their reach,
    And then in terror and amaze
    We clung to braces and to stays,
And shuddering beheld the wreck
Of everything about the deck,
    Exposed to constant blows and shocks
    From loosened booms and falling blocks;
The sturdy topmasts writhed and bent,
Stout shrouds were from their dead-eyes rent,
    The massy timbers of the hull
    Groaned audibly through every lull
Or ebb of conflict; still the rush
Of winds pursued each transient hush,
    Until we drove with scarce a mast
    Full at the mercy of the blast!

"That night—a day—another night,
With short cessations of the fight,
    We stood the brunt of wind and wave,
    With promise of a speedy grave—
A time of terror and of grief
Almost surpassing man's belief,
    Of ceaseless effort to maintain
    A foothold on the reeling main,

Pitched, tossed and tumbled, with the cries
Of mates, swept from before our eyes,
  From time to time arising out
  Of that wild elemental rout—
Borne crying to a restless grave,
While none could stretch a hand to save.

"The rising sun one lovely morn
Looked on a black hulk scarred and worn,
  Slow rolling in the quiet wave
  That soon was to become her grave;
And us—us four, the weary few
Remaining of her gallant crew—
  But four—the captain and his child,
  The hardy boatswain Alfred Wilde,
Myself—and we were all—afloat
On ocean in an open boat.

IV.

"Long in that sea of liquid gold
The wreck of that proud vessel rolled,
  As loath to leave the brilliant day
  And pass to unknown scenes away;
Forevermore to blindly creep
Through mazes of the nether deep;

To grope in mystery and fear
O'er sunken isles and hemisphere;
Bound to a cold and fearful dream
Unbroken by a single beam
From joy-bestowing worlds that tread
Their shining circles overhead;
Rebelling 'gainst the strange decree
That bade her 'scape an angry sea,
Outride the storm of nights and days
'Midst thunder's clash and lightning's blaze,
At last to vanish from the scene
When all is quiet and serene.

" Like some intoxicated beast
Who reels and staggers from the feast,
And moans in his dyspeptic mood,
O'er heavy with rich wine and food,
The helpless monster heaved and rolled,
Laughed at by mocking tongues of gold,
While flags of hemp and tattered sail
Streamed round her in the playful gale
With bated breath and anguish keen
We waited for another scene,
The second in that tragedy.
No human genius could supply—

When suddenly a change! the wreck
Stopped as a steed by sudden check,
   Or as a quarry when the pack
   Has closed around upon his track—
Fixed as a rooted rock that stands
Alone in wide and silent lands,
   A moment, then a shudder came
   That shook her worn and feeble frame,
A tremor as of fear or cold
That ran along her timbers old,
   And then there struggled up a cry
   As from a soul in agony,
Wrung from her overburdened breast
By alien elements oppressed;
   Then, while the waves seemed to rejoice,
   And hail her fate with gleeful voice,
We rose involuntarily
With heads bared reverentially,
   While each heart beat a sad adieu
   As for a comrade tried and true,
On whom some mad and dumb disease
Exerts its deadly energies;
   Stood still as images of stone
   Misplaced and left to drift alone,
   Forgotten—lost—heeded by none,

Saw foot by foot the waves encroach,
Impatient at fate's slow approach;
  Saw the sad hulk by sure degrees
  Sink low and lower in the seas,
'Till o'er the broken bulwarks poured
The eager and impatient horde,
  To join the prisoned waves compressed
  Within the dying monster's breast—
A mingled tide that surged and rolled
With noise like fog-bells faintly tolled—
  A plunge—a struggle—a rebound
  Of parted waves—a gurgling sound,
A close fierce grapple smothered in
A reeling caldron's foam and din,
  A trembling motion round the pole,
  A smoothing over of the whole,
And then the happy waves danced by
With naught between them and the sky.

"A hush fell on us like a wave
Of silence wafted from the grave,
  A sense of loneliness and dread
  That sunk upon our hearts like lead,
A gloom that not the tropic day
With all its splendor could allay,

A sadness that the liquid swell
Of ocean harps could not dispel—
A shade—a ghost of ugly hue
That quite obscured the mental view,
  While all the air was softly stirred
  As by the wing of a phantom bird.

"We sank back in our little space,
A pall each heart, a shroud each face,
  Each cold hand holding in its clasp
  A hand as cold—a deathly grasp.

V.

"The golden chariot of day
Passed on its noiseless wheels away,
  And following upon its rear
  Came twilight's army creeping near;
Advancing slowly, stealthily,
Its mottled footprints marked the sea,
  And sweeping onward down the west
  Left us to meet that darker guest
And to prepare as best we might
Some shelter from the dews of night,
  Those exhalations charged with bane
  That rise from the o'erheated main,

As fatal as the prison beam
The full moon sheds on those who dream
 Unsheltered 'neath her mystic spell, -
 And wake to find their brains a hell.

" Stowed in a locker safe and sound
A fragment of a jib we found,
 Also an awning and a shred
 Of black tarpaulin ; these we spread,
 The awning stretching overhead,
And with the broken pieces found
We housed a little space around,
 And made a cabin for our charge
 In the after portion of the barge,
Divided from us by a screen
Of ample breadth that hung between,
 And when this pleasant task was o'er
 We looked into our little store
Of poor provisions which our care
Saved from the wreck for future fare,
 Food scarce sufficient to sustain
 Life through five days, should life remain ;
A few small cans of navy meat
 (Half cooked already by the heat),

A can of crackers, snugly stored
(To keep from crawling overboard),
And that was all ; but oh, more dear
To sea-worn souls than lordly cheer !
A beaker of pure water, cold
As ever came from vessel's hold !
With grateful hearts we blessed the fare
And took each man a scanty share,
But not till *she*, the first and best,
Had eaten of the tenderest,
And with a bright word and smile
Withdrawn from us a little while.

" And now the sentries of the sky
Were slyly taking post on high,
As up the clear ethereal arch
The shining hosts commenced their march,
Each brilliant band to take its place
Among the glories of its race,
As southwest winds with gentle force
Urged us upon our lonely course,
Set by those constant guides which God
Has set above the wanderer's road.

" It was arranged that I should keep
The early watch, for I could not sleep

From utter wretchedness of heart,
  And fears that I feared to impart—
The awful fear that *she* must share
The fate that threatened us, whose stare
  I fancied oft upon us bent
  Already with its dire intent,
In spite of every effort made
To throw the phantom in the shade—
  To rout it and supply its place
  With forms of loveliness and grace.
And so when gentle sleep had laid
Her hand upon each brave comrade
  I sat upon my quiet post,
  Watching the while the heavenly host!
But wondering in my troubled mind
If *she* a sweet repose could find,
  Or whether in deep loneliness
  She sat and brooded our distress,
When suddenly, as if from out
Some star along the brilliant route,
  An angel clothed in light had stept
  To walk the world while mortals slept,
With noiseless step and anxious mein
Stole to my side my Eveline,

And with a look of trust and love
That would have graced a saint above,
Yet saddened somewhat by a hue
Of secret grief that struggled through,
Settled as softly down by me
As weary sea bird 'neath the lee
Of some rough rock when wind and sea
Are striving for the mastery—
Without a word—without a sign
Save what those dear eyes spake to mine.

" Too full of blessed love to speak,
I stooped and kissed her lily cheek,
While one white hand I caught and prest
In silent rapture to my breast,
That she might feel the mighty force
Of passion smothered at its source—
The passion that had once betrayed
Itself o'erpowering and unstayed.
And thus for hours did we sit there,
Nor with a whisper stirred the air,
But holding each a consciousness
Of some o'erburdening distress—
Each knowing in the breast of each
Affliction lay too deep for speech,

By silent mutual consent
Left to pursue its own event.

" Till oft repeated clasp and kiss
Had plunged us in a dream of bliss
   Sat we.   We heeded not the song
   That trilled the tumbling waves along,
Nor heeded in our rapt heart-charm
Those dark and boding shapes of harm
   That gathered round us dull and dumb,
   Forerunners of some woe to come.
Great hungry sharks two fathoms long
Swam round us in a growing throng,
   And eyed us with dull frightful eyes,
   As marking each his future prize.
Still, though our eyes could watch them glide
Like constant guardians by our side,
   Those dark portentious things did seem
   But harmless creatures of a dream,
As strangely infinitely far
As beings of the fancy are,
   So deep were we in love's blind trance—
   So lost to time and fate and chance.

VI.

" Oh, comrades! 'tis a fearful thing,
This lonesome long sea-suffering—

These burning, thirsting, famished days
Lost in the ocean's mingled ways;
Blown like a feather to and fro
By tides that come and tides that go!
　These nights of sleepless agony
　Looking for sign in sky or sea,
For sign in sky with dread and fear
Lest some storm-token should appear
　For sign in sea of sail or shore
　To wing the famished hope once more;
This earnest and continuous prayer
Amidst distortion and despair,
　For water! water! blessed drink,
　Of which 'tis maddening to think!
To drown the awful thirst that burns
Like a soul that unto sin returns—
　All desolate and dying while
　The calm stars mock us with their smile.

" Had we been strong men one and all
Trained for the worst that could befall,
When fate had sent us to the wall—
　Had suffering of nature been
　The only terrors known or seen,
We could unflinching to the close,
Have borne the body's pains and throes—

Could have sustained them to the end
And died with friend embracing friend,
Or hopeless of a will to save
Have sought at once a handy grave,
Consigning torture to the wave.

But oh! how fearful when combined
With constant anguish of the mind,
Itself more terrible by far
Than pains and ills of body are;

When quick imagination fed
By sorrow's bitter wine and bread
Conspires with every other ill
The draughts of madness to distil,
While circumstance with joy intense,
Stirs up the gross ingredients,
Till terror seizes on the bowl
And pours it foaming o'er the soul.

" Who would not have been crazed with care
When one so innocent and fair,
So dearly sweet—so fondly true,
So lovely and so loving too,
As she, my patient Eveline,
Was forced upon that desperate scene;
Torn rudely from her woman's place
To meet what stout men shake to face;

To feel midst frenzy and despair
What manhood would have shrieked to bear ?
  This was the awful thought that stung
  Each heart and every mind unstrung;
This was the tireless bird that preyed
On souls not easily dismayed,
  O'ershadowing with gloomy wings
  The bosom's pure refreshing springs.

" But while for her we inly pined
She seemed both patient and resigned,
  And strove by every winning art
  To make the mind forget its smart,
Told cheerful tales to cheer us up,
And sweetened many a bitter cup ;
  And while her happy fancy wrought
  Its charming romances, it taught
That lesson which so many spurn,
The hardest for a man to learn,
  That woman, spite her tenderness,
  Her grief and pity for distress,
 Her lovable and loving arts,
  Those outward proofs of mobile hearts ;
    Her infinite resource of mood,
    By sterner minds misunderstood,

When stung by fate's or passion's heat,
Or forced to danger's front can meet
   With more than manly fortitude
   Misfortune's many-handed brood,
And with her pure strength put to shame
All mean traducers of her name.

"The time toiled tediously away
And dim night broadened into day;
   Then broad day narrowed down to night,
   And yet no sign—no sail in sight
No blessed moment of release
From gnawing cares, no spell of peace
   'Midst all this outward smilingness,
   This nature in her gayest dress,
This wealth of oriental peace
That seemed too heavenly to cease;
   No change; but day succeeding day
   Still saw us on our hopeless way,
Each formal day and night that passed
But repetition of the last,
   Until the sun had done his march
   Four times through the empyreal arch,
Until the moon four times had come
And looked upon us dull and dumb,

Until the fifth unhallowed dawn,
And then our wretched food was gone.

VII.

"But I must hasten with my tale,
Or else impatience will prevail;
   Must make an effort to condense
   My yarn or lose my audience;
For did my narrative aspire
To give each scene and act entire
   That helped to make the matchless play
   Which I endeavor to portray;
Should I endeavor to impart
To each its just degree of art,
   This simple tale would grow as long
   And tedious as an epic song,
And ere I reached my middle point
Would twist attention out of joint.
   A verbal tale devoid of art
   Should echo to the hearer's heart,
Move with the measure and the force
With which the blood performs its course,
   Accompany the pulse along,
   And yours is rapid now and strong.

VIII.

" Methinks I see him plainly now,
A dark sombrero on his brow ;
   His close-curled Saxon locks—his eyes
   Deep blue and humorously wise ;
His sunbrowned face, whose quiet smile
Told of a nature free from guile ;
   His ruddy cheeks and brilliant flash
   Of teeth behind a blonde mustache ;
His heavy chin and bronzen neck,
A sculpture without flaw or fleck ;
   His body's perfect symmetry,
   His calm demeanor, manners free—
As fine a type of manly grace
As e'er enriched the Grecian race,
   And yet a thorough ocean child,
   The hardy boatswain Alfred Wilde.

" It was the strangest thing to all
That *he* should be the first to fall ;
   'Twas what we could not understand
   That *he* was chosen of our band
The first to launch upon the sea
Of an unknown eternity.

'Twas strange that while there yet remained
In the water cask a drop undrained,
His spirits held their wonted flow
Nor rose above nor sunk below;
But when the final draught was drunk
His humor failed—his body shrunk,
His speech grew surly in its tone
And he preferred to be alone,
Then, growing timid and afraid,
His words in mazy channels strayed,
Which ended in a common sea
Of strangest grief invariably,
From out whose depths of mingled woes
At times a storm of curses rose
Too terrible for man to hear
Without a thrill of mortal fear.

" But all this came to terminate
In 6ne grand master-stroke of fate,
That fell more forcibly because
It seemed averse to nature's laws;
Because it lopped our staunchest limb
With the nest of hopes that clung to him—
Tore the gigantic sprout away
And spared the young unseasoned spray;

Cut off a fine vitality
Formed by the medicinal sea,
  And passed by in immortal scorn
  The aged and the tender-born.

" 'Twas on a night—a pure sad night,
And we lay drowned in seas of light
  Poured by the moon the waves along
  As they sang low their evening song ;
The southwest wind had ceased to sing
And slumbered 'neath his folded wing ;
  So we had furled our little sail
  To wait the freshening of the gale,
If we indeed should ever feel
Another billow lift our keel.
  My precious fading Eveline
  Reposed apace behind the screen,
The captain, worn with pain and care,
Sat in the bows with his despair ;
  I, in a mockery of rest,
  Was leaning 'gainst a pistol chest,
While Wilde sat looking o'er the side
With wide eyes fixed upon the tide,
  Watching the ugly shapes below
  Noiselessly gliding to and fro—

Seemed in his contemplative trance
Interpreting each frightful glance
   Shot from those still and boding eyes,
   So liquid black and fiendish wise—
Coldly engaged in studying
For the very madness of the thing
   The structure of those deadly orbs
   Whose power imperils and absorbs.
I let my heavy eye-lids close,
And passed with a nervous doze,
   Painful and plagued ; but by and by
   I was awakened by a cry—
An awful yell that drove the blood
Back to my heart in a hurried flood,
   And in that solitude serene
   Cut to the quick like weapon keen—
Filled for a breath the startled ear
With its terrific note of fear,
   And then without an echo fell
   Flat on the surface of the swell.

" I leapt upon my feet and saw
A sight that struck me dumb with awe,
   A spectacle that chained me there
   With the still fetters of despair,

Until my dazed and reeling brain
Was master of itself again,
  And then came drifting o'er my mind
  A sense of humor undefined,
A wave of silent laughter blown
Through temples lying spoiled and prone—
  A sudden broad and genial beam
  That made the whole transaction seem
  The solemn waggery of a dream.

" He stood with body backward thrown,
As rigid as a man of stone,
  And on his lips and in his eyes,
  A spirit lurked in shocking guise,
A sign most perfectly expressed
Of some fierce torture at the breast,
  Some boundless fantasy of brain
  That clothed him with a garb insane,
And sunk the chin, relaxed the cheek,
With terror that he might not speak.
  But what was that before him there,
  That thin and wavering thing of air
  The moon shone through with yellow glare—
That formless fluctuating light
So warm and luminously bright ?

Pshaw ! but a mist before the eye,
A cloud upon the visual sky !
What else but that I'd like to know
One moment could deceive me so !
I smiled with unbelieving lips
And pressed two icy finger tips
Upon my aching lids, and then
Looked up with confidence again—
But lo ! the cloud had taken form
And darkened like a growing storm,
Had formed proportions and a plan
And stood the semblance of a man ;
Its look—its face I could not see,
The figure's back was turned to me,
But I could note the well-known style
And bearing of its frame the while,
Its every aspect did denote
A man-of-war's-man well afloat.
But suddenly as in alarm
The phantom raised its long right arm,
Quick beckoned in the boatswain's face
And then withdrew a single pace,
And he, without a sign or word,
Or moan or whisper to be heard,

Moved with it to the gunwale where
They stood as if in doubt or prayer
A moment, and the next the wave
Enclosed them in a common grave.

" That night and the succeeding day
Wrapped in a death-like trance she lay,
So purely fair, so sweetly weak,
With lovely languor on her cheek,
With dreamy sweetness in her eyes
And on her lips unuttered sighs,
So pearly beautiful ! O, sight
That brought a lost and deep delight !
O vision of such happiness
As lover mad alone can guess !
O glimpse of pure unearthly love
Vouchsafed to mortals from above—
Immortal triumph of the heart
O'er every earthly thought or part,
Bright breaking of celestial day
Into a prison-house of clay !

" The stricken parent pale and wild
In tearless grief hung o'er his child—
Sat like a frozen image there
Communing with his fixed despair—

Bound in a grief too deep for speech
His parent's love his only leech;
  Sat there so long—sat there so fast,
  I thought to rouse him up at last—
I spoke—he answered not a word,
I spoke again—he never stirred,
  I gently pushed him with my hand,
  And still he would not understand,
And then persisting in my way
I took his hand . . . a shadow gray
  Had slid between us stealthily,
  So I desisted with a sigh,
And ere the moon had set the sea
Had closed on all but her and me.

" And next my mind grew wild and lost
In ways that ever crossed, re-crossed,
  And turned and twisted in and out
  By many a dark and reckless route,
Through scenes of every shade and hue
That longer seen the wilder grew;
  Then in a region vast, so vast,
  So lonely, voiceless to the last;
A breathless chaos wide, so wide,
So desolate and dead beside,

A space so destitute and gray
  It seemed the grave of life and day—
All lifeless save a spotless thing
Soaring high up on balanced wing,
    The likeness of a bird of snow,
    That winged its upward way sublime and slow.

" I never clearly knew what space
Of time we lingered in that place ;
    I know not, yet it scarcely may
    Have been for more than a single day ;
I've always thought it scarcely might
Have been for more than another night,
    For human nature hardly could
    For a longer season have withstood
The awful pressure brought to bear
Upon those human natures there—
    That clime in which my spirit dwelt
    No change of time has ever felt.

" But there were intervals of change,
When flashed across my mental range
    A transient intermittent ray
    Which in that vast had lost its way,
Emitting brief uncertain gleams,
Now here, now there, in broken beams,

But e'er presenting to my view
A face that more familiar grew
The more its presence haunted me,
Until at last it came to be
A constant guest, the only thing
In all my world that took not wing,
The only thing that did abide
Amidst that region wild and wide—
That likeness of a bird of snow
That kept its way sublime and slow.
I had this consciousness alone,
Though dim through an eclipse it shone,
That in my dire extremity
She was ministering to me.

IX.

" At last I woke, as one would wake
Who had been buried by mistake,
And who had struggled through the gloom
And torment of a living tomb,
Till in exhaustion and in dread
He lay like one more truly dead,
Yet scarcely less than dead when day
Broke brilliant through his prison clay,
Recalling him from death and night
To walk the world in life and light.

" I rose—I looked—I closed my eyes—
I looked again in deep surmise,
  For how was this ?   I shook—I feared—
  The sea—its scenes had disappeared,
And where the horizon had shone
Were four white walls like walls of stone ;
  I flung a glance toward the sky—
  A lofty ceiling met my eye—
Ah, yes ! I see ! another phase
Of my disease perverts my gaze !
  Content with this solution I
  Sank on my pillow with a sigh.
Was this a pillow ? strange to see
A pillow in the boat with me !
  Is this the boat in which I lie ?
  Am I myself, or who am I ?
Sure I'm awake, I see—I feel
My brain is clear and sharp as steel—
  Good grace ! is that *my* face within
  Yon mirror on the wall ? how thin—
How white and wasted of its flesh
That used to be so full and fresh !
  Are those *my* eyes reflected there,
  Meeting my gaze with hollow stare ?

Well, it was curious at best,
And I could not perceive the jest,
So, feeling weak I sank again to rest.

"It was a hospital, they said,
Whither, a madman, I'd been led
 Some months before, and by the hands
 Of men who came from foreign lands,
Some seamen who found me afloat
In ocean in an open boat,
 With one female companion who,
 Though dying, had found strength to do
All which in that place might be done
To aid a loved and stricken one;
 Who, at the moment of relief,
 Yielded to suffering and grief,
And lay for many a day and week
Without the power to think or speak;
 Receiving every tender care
 'Twas possible to meet with there,
Until the crisis passed at length
And she recovered health and strength.
 But I, a gentle madman still,
 Could not be brought to yield to skill,
Which, when all remedies were spent,
Pronounced my madness permanent.

So when at last the vessel lay
At anchor in a native bay,
I was conveyed with others where
I could receive more constant care,
    And there proficient men had found
    At least a hope to make me sound.

" And this was all that they could tell,
Nor learned I aught of what befell
    Her whom I loved; whither she turned
    When my revolting fate she learned,
Although I left no means untried
To ascertain—sought far and wide,
    Roamed like a spirit up and down
    Through seaside city vast and town;
Pursued my ceaseless inquiry
Where'er men dwelt beside the sea,
    Until my name and tale were known
    Wherever ocean winds have blown—
For months and years, and all in vain—
No far voice answered from the main,
    No tidings came of her or hers,
    No answer from our rescuers,
Not even an illusive ray
To cheer me for a single day

Rose *ignis fatuus*-like from out
That marsh of mystery and doubt.

" O, mournful, mournful fate !   O heart,
Shot through with disappointment's dart !
   Doomed like a guilty exiled thing
   To walk the world a sorrowing !
O, sacred passion marked for years
To battle with life's wasting fears,
Yet brave in sorrow, beautiful in tears !

X.

" Years passed and I became again
A wanderer from the homes of men;
   Bowed with a hopeless misery
   I sought again the friendly sea
   And found at last some sympathy;
Wept first my sorrows on its breast,
And rose comforted and caressed—
   Rose with a calmer mind, a gaze
   Bent hopefully on future days;
A lighter heart—a purer soul,
And passions under calm control,
   And with a strong presentiment
   Of some approaching glad event

To recompense me for the past,
And give me life and peace at last.

" Eighteen full years up to a day
Since my shipwreck had wound away;
   Eighteen complete illusions whirled
   From off the great reel of the world,
Rolled with their vast loads of decay
Down old oblivion's sloping way.
   I said 'twas eighteen years, I say
   'Twas eighteen years up to a day,
And I again looked on that scene,
That sky, that sun, those seas serene—
   As calm—as beautiful as when
   Their beauty so deceived my ken;
When other eyes were there to drink
Their charms, and other lips to link
   Their scattered gems into a chain
   Of beauty coiling round the brain—
There found ourselves without a breeze
Rolled in those golden Indian seas,
   Becalmed upon the sultry tide,
   With sea-dust glistening far and wide;
When suddenly arose a hail
From a lookout—' A sail! a sail!'

And every eye was turned upon
The faint and hazy horizon,
To catch the ever-welcome gleam
Of sun on canvas. On our beam—
  Our starboard beam, with glass to aid
  My sight, a little speck I made,
A brilliant point so far away
At times I almost lost the ray,
When 'man the barge!' I heard the captain say.

"I did not pause to question why
Such haste; but in the captain's eye
  I read an intense interest
  That was not otherwise expressed.
His glass, more powerful than mine,
Had shown him some unusual sign,
  Some point about that sail which he
  Did not communicate to me;
And I chose not in any sense
To worm into his confidence,
  So I said not a word at all,
  But helped to tend the barge's fall,
And as she plashed into the tide
Took my position by his side.
  Then all impatiently the boys
  Pulled lustily and without noise—

Pulled and perspired until at last,
After a goodly distance past,
    The object of our search appeared
    Close on our bow, and as we neared
An influence of awe and fear
Seemed to pervade the atmosphere,
    An air so odorous of death
    It nearly took away my breath,
And made a sinking sickness fall
Upon my heart, and shook a pall,
    Torn from the coffin of the past,
    Around my senses waning fast—
Drew it so close about my brain
It made me nervously insane,
    And caused all things around to seem
    The memory of an ancient dream;
As near and nearer we advanced
This strange sensation was enhanced—
    But hold! what sight is here revealed!
    What! do I dream with lids unsealed?
I shake myself and look once more,
But all these things I've seen before!
    My thoughts flash back across the years,
    And there this self-same scene appears!

My memory deceives me not,
This seems indeed the very spot,
    And this the sky, and this the sea
    That still reflect that memory.
Great heaven! these wonders but increase!
What starved and dying souls are these
    That greet our eyes all wonder-wide
    As we swiftly shoot to that vessel's side?
That exile female form so fair
I'm almost sure I've seen somewhere,
    That pale sweet face I too have seen—
    My God! my God! my Eveline!
The same dear love of other days
In everything! I gasp—I gaze—
    Yes, there she stands before my ken,
    As young and beautiful as when
We were alone upon the sea
And she arose and tended me,
    When I was mad and did not know
    Aught but the love that loved me so!
Yes, there she stands above a form
Which the quick life has ceased to warm,
    A clod—a sod—a thing of death
    O'er which she bends with bated breath!

But I no longer could restrain
The forward impulse of my brain,
  The mastering sense of mystery,
  That drew me on impulsively,
I cried out like a wounded thing
And cleared the cutter with a spring—
  Leapt like a panther from my seat
  And landed lightly on my feet
Beside the living and her dead,
And spoke in haste; she raised her head,
  And met me with a pair of eyes
  So full of sorrowful surprise,
So full of speechless questionings
And a hundred other mournful things,
  My heart leapt in a quick response
  And bound me to her cause at once,
But while my lips strove to repeat
She wilted flower-like at my feet.

XI.

" And now I have but to relate
How kindly my attendent fate
Smoothed out the wrinkles of his hate;
  How my life-path led quickly out
  Of that thick-tangled land of doubt,

And in among the pleasant ways
Of peaceful nights and balmy days:
   Encircled by that magic ring
   From which all perfect pleasures spring ;
No more to pierce the middle dim
Of years, but lightly tread their rim,
   Skirt life's delightful yellow verge
   Where virtue's paths at last emerge ;
Where passion's hot mischievous blaze
Melts into faith's refulgent haze,
   And storms and tumults of the past
   Beat faint and far and cease at last.

" Strange was the story that was told
When sickness had released his hold
   Upon her tender frame, and health
   And youthful bloom their pristine wealth
Restored; and harmony and song,
Rang from sweet heart-strings silenced long,
   And life and light danced in her ee
   The life and light that were for me—
For with my history she learned
To love the soul that strongly yearned
   Through years and years of blasting dearth
   And yet retained its wealth and worth.

" I'm now an old and stricken man,
Whose life has nigh fulfilled its plan,
   But there survives through all these years,
   Bright from their joys and ills and tears,
The marvel and the mystery
With which I heard her history—
   That part, I mean, closed by the line
   Where hers became as one with mine,
That part of suffering and grief
Almost transcending man's belief,
   And as your eager looks betray
   Your wish to hear without delay,
I'll haste to render you the key
Of access to this mystery,
   Although the facts thereof befell
   Later than what remains to tell.

" When eighteen years had passed away
From our unhappy shipwreck day,
   There were enacted o'er again,
   Upon that far-off Indian main,
   Those very scenes of gloom and pain
Whose crude recital moved you so—
The wreck and its succeeding woe,
   Recall that portion of my tale
   Beginning with the midnight gale,

And follow on to the event
When my wild soul a wandering went;
  Recall each incident inwrought
  In that bewildering war of thought;
Review each episode that went
To form that cursed imprisonment;
  Remember every scene and act
  In that wild tragedy in fact;
And then consolidate the whole
In one huge horror of the soul,
  And you possess her history
  As she related it to me.
Though strange and startling it may seem,
And like the substance of a dream,
  These scenes enacted in my sight,
  Long years ere she beheld the light,
In their minutest details came
To her in manner just the same;
  By some strange law of fate it passed,
  Both streams were in one channel cast;
So strict—precise in every sense,
And perfect the coincidence,
  That only one event befell
  Unknown in the original,

And that, the last that did betide,
When the ill-fated lover died.

" Strange was the tale, and who would guess
That after all I should possess
   My precious long-lost love of old
   With all its azure and its gold ;
Untarnished by the dust of years,
Unwasted by life's wasting fears !
   But so it was, my Eveline,
   Alone, an orphan, having seen
Her fated lover borne away
To linger out life's dismal day,
   As she supposed, in mindless gloom,
   More bitter than an early tomb,
After a fitting time was spent
In giving pent-up sorrow vent,
   And months of quietness and calm
   Had rendered her restoring balm,
Yielded to the unperjured art
Of one who sought her hand and heart,
   And if her heart was hopeless flown
   The honor of her hand alone ;
Leant quiet ear to the appeal
Of a warm nature true as steel,

And to his earnest suit replied
That if he could be satisfied
With what of love remained to her
That willingly would she confer
On him, her friend and rescuer,
   Her friend—the only one below
   Who knew her griefs, or cared to know.
They wed, and never o'er life's sea
Did drift two lives more peacefully;
   And if her early losses pressed
   At times upon her matron breast,
Or if a yearning for the old
First love that never could grow cold,
   With sadness, like a garb divine,
   Enfolded her, 'twas all, no sign,
Or outward trace was ever seen
Of a regret for what had been;
   And when unto her charge was given
   The third bright angel fresh from heaven,
She slept in death's forgetfulness
And earth possessed one angel less;
   Departed and unconsciously
   Bequeathed immortal wealth to me—
A perfect joyous little elf,
The image of her former self;

The bright embodiment divine
Of all the love that had been mine :
A passion of celestial birth
Permitted to remain on earth ;
  A jewel of unchanging ray
  Preserved in casket of sweet clay,
For one who sought with woes untold
To clasp it in the former mould.
  And thus I won my Eveline,
  The sweetest girl that e'er was seen,
Turned to outwitted death and smiled,
And clasped the mother in the child."

SPRAY.

A SEA TROUBLE.

BEYOND the light-house, far asea,
  The wind and waves are quarrelling
  In angry tones about something
That is a mystery to me.

Low down along the threatening South
  I hear the breakers wildly curse,
  Each moment growing worse and worse—
I see them foaming at the mouth.

Some faint far lightnings flash and die
　On the black border of the bay,
　In passionate and hateful play
Like amorous angers of an eye.

The sails lie o'er on their sides,
　Warped by the inward blowing wind
　That rides with furious rush behind,
And drives them through opposing tides.

Gaunt shapes are stalking overhead—
　Gigantic squadrons on their march
　Through heaven's overshadowing arch
With stealthy and avenging tread.

They ever move me painfully,
　And I do wish that they would end—
　These strifes I cannot comprehend;
For thought is mystery to me
And these bring thought and mystery.

TO EVA.

THY smile could wring from senseless clay
  The sweetest song that e'er was sung,
And call from darkness into day
  A soul to lyric madness strung,
To twine, with heart and mind aflame,
Unfading wild-flowers round thy name!

Thy scorn could summon from the past
  The genius of old tragedy
With thoughts like the continuous blast
  Of headlong tempests on the sea,
Such as old Marlowe felt of yore
Break on his life's unquiet shore.

A wish of thine could rend the mesh
  That fetters young idea's wing,
And make the empire of the flesh
  Subservient to creation's spring,
While she erects o'er reason's throne
A burning kingdom all thy own.

Thy swift thoughts span the circling sea
  (How beat these joy-throbs on my brain !),
And straight I feel an ecstacy—
  A sweetly-agonizing pain
Pierce down into the secret cells,
Where love with all her mystery dwells,

  A burning hunger of the lips,
An intense energy of heart,
  An iron hand that tightly grips
My brain with unrelenting smart,
  A rushing of the blood along,
  A burst of wild barbaric song!

In midnight watches on the sea,
  In island city's gleaming walls,
Thy tireless spirit comes to me
  In tempests and in bacchanals,
Sowing in furrows of my breast
The quick seeds of a wild unrest.

On shores where years have piled their wrecks,
  And piled and heaped them o'er again,
Till one high moss-grown barrier checks
  The marching legions of the main,
Thy searching spirit, life-endued,
Did people all my solitude !

Whene'er I pierce, by land or sea,
   To fiery isles or tropic lakes,
Thy still thought ever follows me
   And on my antique fancy breaks—
Breaks up the primal gloom of soul
That otherwise would all control.

If, while thy endless chain I wear,
   And feel it tightening link by link,
Another aspiration dare
   To mount above my passion's brink
It soars but to reveal to me
Thy power and *my* infirmity.

Could mortals claim but one delight
   And right of choice to me were given,
To bide a saint in spotless white,
   Or cling to thee and forfeit heaven
I'd quaff thy cup of lotus bloom,
And plunge me into heathen gloom.

LOVE'S REVIVAL.

OH, Florence ! Florence ! do you know
   What a sweet pleasure of surprise
   Lurks in the depths of your dear eyes ?
How in their shy and winy glow
I feel my heart blood swell and flow,
   And hear its old instinctive cries ?

Those hot sweet cries I thought were hushed
   And dumb, drowned down to rise no more
   With their fierce clamor, as before,
When youth's great torrent roared and rushed,
Till one too vivid heart was crushed,
   And one was stricken to its core.

I might have known—I might have guessed
   That love dies not so easily
   In tropic hearts, but secretly
Will nurse the deep wound in his breast,
Regaining in his death-like rest
   His wonted fierce vitality.

Till some fond phrase of eye or lip
  Thrills in between his prison bars,
  Then vanish ancient wounds and scars,
His rozy limbs their fetters slip,
Pride withers in his lusty grip,
  While wisdom flies to join the stars.

Ah, foolish human brain! to think
  To conquer with your wise conceits
  The darling rogue who ever cheats
The reason of his boasted scope;
Ah, silly pride! how now you grope—
  Where now your pure exalted seats?

Oh, Florence! Florence! what have you
  Been doing to this heart of mine—
  What wondrous work of art divine
Has your bright fancy found to do!
This golden mist I see you through
  Is sure some deep-wrought charm of thine!

No faint and languid breeze of sighs
  Is it that stirs this current so,
  No pleasant airs that lightly blow
'Neath amorous suns and smiling skies,
But some still force that has its rise
  In hidden caverns far below.

I feel its power—I pause—I yield—
　　I toss a kiss up to the sun
　　To seal the victory he's won;
I ground my sorry lance and shield,
And stretch my bare arms from the field,
　　For you to slip the fetters on.

You've won; but never yet so strange
　　A captive as you'll find in me,
　　So true—so false; so tame—so free;
So blessed—so cursed with every change
Of mood within the mind's wide range,
　　And yet so fixed in constancy.

You held the straws for me to draw—
　　I drew—the shortest, let it stay,
　　I'll not cry "unfair" any way;
One more content you never saw
To bide by love's delightful law,
　　Sweet tyranny! for aye and aye.

FLORA.

FLORA is a tender flower,
  Growing in the world's broad meadow,
Nursed by summer's sun and shower,
  Clouded never by a shadow.

Flora is a mirthful creature,
  Full of infant rhyme and measure,
Every grace of form and feature
  Eloquent of love and pleasure.

I can scarce believe her mortal,
  But some playful little fairy,
Hovering at life's rosy portal,
  Doubtful if to fly or tarry.

Some delightful angel comer
  Sowing seeds of love before her,
Shedding hope's delightful summer
  O'er the fond hearts that adore her.

Flora's eyes are brown and browner,
  Flora's ways are fresh and rosy,
Blushing health and beauty crown her,
  Flora is a mountain posy.

THE SACRIFICE.

She gives him to the deep with many tears,
  Resigns her darling to the tempter main,
And mingles fervent blessings with her prayers—
  Recalls him oft and kisses him again.

He is hers only; early death has torn
  From her choice care the others ere their hearts
Had grown to wander, or their feet had worn
  The patient earth, or mingled in its marts.

She sees his young heart lives where ocean sweeps,
  His first affection centered in the sea,
And recognizes even while she weeps
  The genius that directs his destiny.

Spurning his toys she sees him seek its side
  And glory in the aspect of its charms;
His fresh thoughts chafing with impatient pride,
  Fierce for the pressure of its reaching arms.

The curious things that it has cast ashore
  She sees him scrutinize with meaning gaze—
The windings of some rare shell to explore,
  He quits his playmates and their thoughtless ways

When tempests stir the ocean up to wrath
  And all the powers are banded to destroy,
High up the rocks on some perilous path
  She sees him stand and fling his arms for joy.

And ofttimes when the waves in pleasant dance
  Brush with light footsteps the enamored sands,
She notes him in imaginative trance,
  His fleet thoughts sailing on to other lands,

And realizes how the irksome chain
  Which binds a free young spirit to enthrall,
In after years may rust into the brain,
  And charge the bosom with its deadly gall.

She muses o'er the tales that man has told
  Of dire disaster and a watery grave,
When chiefest of the bold in vain are bold,
  And valor's soul cannot avail the brave.

Then springs triumphant fancy on the scene,
  And opes her vivid canvas to the eye—
Wrecks, battles, whirlpools, terrors submarine,
  In scenic sections pass exultant by.

" Just God! a portion of Thy spirit burns
  Strong in the bosom of my noble boy—
Oh, keep the jewel bright till it returns
  With added lustre to its crown of joy !

" When tossed by tempests, fearful and alone,
   His brave bark hangs upon destruction's brink,
Oh, calm the storm, or bear him bravely on
   To brighter seas, where no hot whirlpools sink

" And shield him from those tempests of the soul,
   More terrible than storms of ocean are—
The witchery of passion and the bowl
   That drowns the lustre of the brightest star !

" Teach him to drink full deep the grand sad song
   The sad sea sings in its Creator's praise,
And ope his bosom to the angel throng
   That guards the wanderer o'er the ocean ways."

'Tis done ! the ocean, like an eager bride,
   Has drawn the youthful dreamer to its breast ;
There, dreaming his grand dreams, may he abide,
   A poet, wooed, protected and caressed.

WAIFS.

I.

I LOVE to breathe the mountain air,
  And feel my spirit high and free;
I love to linger musing where
  The freeborn streams rush merrily,
  By mossy rock and aged tree;
I love to hear the wild bird fling
  Her notes of rapture through these bowers,
As pausing on her homeward wing
  She fills the air with vocal showers
  'Midst rustling leaves and wakening flowers.

I love to climb the mountain high,
  O'er wooded slope, through deep ravine,
When darkly lowers the summer sky
  Above the gray cliffs dimly seen
  Through ever-shifting waves of green;
To catch the quivering incense borne
  On wings of wayward zephyrs o'er
The valley's wealth of gold-haired corn
  From flowers that bloom along the shore
  Of lakes flushed with the day-god's gore.

I love to stand upon the rock
 And see the tempest pass beneath,
To hear the thunder's rattling shock
 And see the fiery lightning wreath,
 Like weapon flashing from its sheath;
To hear the heavy swollen waves
 Beat at the mountain's granite gates,
While voices from its inner caves,
 Where some imprisoned wind awaits,
 Moan hollow answer to their mates.

I love to thread the deep morass
 That stretches at the mountain's foot,
Through dank and serpent-haunted grass,
 O'er quaking bog and tangled root,
 Where spires of venomed herbage shoot;
And stand at midnight all alone,
 And watch the mystic star-beam glide,
And see the moon's refulgent zone
 Reflected in the listless tide
 That floats round islands wild and wide.

Plunged in the city's noisy whirl,
 Where human life beats like a sea
On which no ship her sails may furl
 Because of rocks upon the lee
 That loom up grim and threateningly,

I love to note the race of arts
　　And sciences and industries,
And grasp the lesson each imparts,
　　And shape them into prophecies
　　Of future great consistencies.

But oh, the grand mysterious sea!
　　My muse's most abiding theme,
The source of mighty joy to me,
　　The substance of the grandest dream
　　That ever stirred the mind's deep stream;
'Tis here, amidst the whirlwind's reel,
　　The strife of dark gigantic foes,
Nerved by a high and wild appeal,
　　I reach, and as truth's gates unclose,
　　Grasp solace for my ills and woes.

'Twas in these budding isles of green
　　That bloom along the southern foam,
Where central summer reigns serene
　　And savage beauty has its home,
　　And scorns to toil nor cares to roam;
'Twas here, wooed by the lotus-breath
　　Of deep and languor-loving seas,
I caught the bird that tastes not death
　　And made it love the northern breeze,
　　To cheer me in my hours of ease.

I love the beautiful and rare—
The strong, the deep, and darkly free—
My ever-changing moods declare
   My spirit's strange inconstancy,
   A sad but sweet infirmity;
Some dear fair face will charm awhile,
   And paint me love in crimson hue,
And trouble me with frown or smile,
   When some huge shape looms on my view,
   With tumbling thunders breaking through.

II.

Go, bring us coffee, dainty cigarettes,
   And luscious fruits, the guava and the pine;
Fetch tender fish caught in soft silken nets
   Webbed by the hands of dark-haired girls divine,
   Who sit and weave in these deep shades of thine;
To-day the ocean wanderer shall be free,
   His ship rides idly on the painted tide—
Forgotten he the dangers of the sea,
   And the vexations that the spirit tried;
   In thy endearing arms, my island bride!

The weary days are over, and the sun
   Of thy warm love shines out across the track—

The dreary track o'er which my bark has run
  Since on this paradise I turned my back
  And went down into ocean's hollows black,
Swift-running sands had brought the time of toil,
  And toil is good that cometh in its turn;
All these sweet draughts of pleasure are its spoil,
  For these I strove—this dear reward to earn—
  Full well I filled my task, for fee I burn.

And thou hast waited too a weary spell,
  Gazing adown the golden track of morn,
Gazing while eve upon the waters fell
  And in the heavens hung up her silver horn,
  To see a sail of shifting shadows born;
And then, perhaps, as none led up the steep
  To tell of sea-worn wanderer's return,
Those eyes so brilliant now first learned to weep,
  That careless bosom first to fondly yearn
  Beyond thine isle with hopes that made thee burn.

The dream is weaving that shall cover me
  Surround me—hide me from the outer world
Where thou art not; my soul is full of thee,
  And where thy mystic golden chain lies curled
  The wings that felt the tempest shall be furled;

Love, we will feast on all that nature gives,
   And drunk with kisses feel no more of earth;
Plunged in the burning wild where passion lives
   We'll call an unknown rapture into birth,
   Distilled of love, forgetfulness and mirth.

Haste, dusky boy, and bring an ample share
   Of every sweet this tropic garden grows;
Spread wide our emerald tent with dainty fare,
   And drink in which no maddening demon glows;
   Gold shall reward thee and make light thy woes;
This hour shall wake the senses' bacchanal
   The revel of the emancipated heart,
Long time obedient to duty's call—
   How sweet at last to feel its fetters part,
   And love and feast and song drown every smart!

Love is the wine of youth, and we are young—
   Oh, love! how glorious in this bright clime!
'Twas 'mong such luxuries the cherub sprung
   Resplendent in unwaning summer-time,
   Chambered in blossomed walls of palm and lime;
Can aught less dear than love such cradle know,
   Such richness nurse a sterner infancy?
Lulled on a bosom that doth overflow,

The darling here attains maturity,
Unchilled by winter's stern inclemency.

Thinkest thou his chubby little feet are cold
With such a soft warm carpet everywhere,
Woven in green luxuriance fold in fold,
Matted and knotted with especial care,
And soft and yielding as a couch in air?
Thinkest thou he lacketh an abundant store
Of sweets to hold his joyous blood unspent,
With all this glorious fruitage beading o'er
His leafy canopy profusely blent,
In all the stages of development?

But wine is sweetest taken after toil,
So love is richest after time of pain;
How sweet to feel amidst the mind's turmoil
Its grateful drops fall warm upon the brain,
Recalling its fresh fantasies again;
Here on our yielding couch we'll taste the sweets
That flow spontaneous through this wilderness,
While every zephyr that so fondly greets
The languid sense, inspires the fond caress,
And all the joys that wedded loves possess.

*　　*　　*　　*　　*　　*　　*　　*

Look yonder! at the ocean's open gates
   Stands the resplendent architect of day,
In all the splendor that upon him waits
   When to the court of dawn he takes his way
   To view the world that joys to own his sway;
Before the light of his great golden eye
   Behold the shapeless shadows disappear,
And vapors that lie piled along the sky
   Sink down supine or flee away in fear,
   To hide in dense morasses wet and drear.

See how his gay light flashes on our shore,
   Where lie the little wavelets fast asleep,
Yet murmuring in their slumber o'er and o'er
   As day's dream-images around them creep,
   Weaving a net of sunbeams o'er the deep;
Look how the crescent curve of shining beach
   Is by a million slender shell-wrecks sown,
Their little pilots dead who used to teach
   What course to set when by hot whirlwinds strown,
   And cast away in currents not their own.

When *they* are wrecked no grim old wrecker springs
   Forth from his rocks on wings of canvas borne,
To glut upon the spoil disaster brings,
   As when some prouder barks by tempests torn
   Spread out their treasures on the sands at morn;

No sea can crush their triple ermine walls,
 Or wedge or grind them in the riven rocks;
But desolate within his winding walls
 The gritty little Spartan lies and mocks
 In gradual death all timber-tearing shocks.

Does that bright thing far off against the sky,
 That slowly-drifting fairy-moulded thing,
So like r fair hand waving some one nigh,
 With the light grace of silent beckoning,
 A cooling sense of airy freedom bring?
Does it appear to thy far sight a sail,
 Or anything by human labor wrought?
Nay, keep thy glass, its power would spoil the tale—
 The heavenly bright idea I have caught,
 And hidden in the temple of my thought.

Are not these groves a dream in which we dream?
 A lovelier dream was never dreamed before;
On yon cocoa's green there is a gleam
 Reflected from the ocean's polished floor,
 Expanding from our covert's tap'stried door;
Pluck me yon golden orange from its bough,
 Its wine is sweetest taken from thy hand—
That flamed-winged bird has ceased his rattling now,
 Lightly he hangs upon his bamboo wand
 As if awaiting thy supreme command.

His big round eyes in belts of gaudy hues,
  Filled with amusing wonderment, look down,
His gay head cocked, as if he fears to lose
    One draught thy beauty offers, darling clown!
    So careless-happy though he wears a crown!
His life is one perpetual holiday,
  His love the love that has no after sting;
And he is wondrous wise, too, in his way,
    Can wield a tongue that is unwearying,
    And laugh and chat and flirt his purple wing.

And every tree that blooms or fructifies
  Has its sweet poet lifting up his voice
From heart o'erflowing in such eulogies
    That one is bound to listen and rejoice,
    Forgetting that his lay entreats a choice;
For who has drunk a poet's living song,
  And drunk and drunk till full of wild delight,
And questioned why he sang so well and long,
    Or what inspired his spirit's daring flight
    Beyond the circle of our frailer sight?

Ho! ho! by George! the woods have devils too!
  And hideous little dried-up imps they seem,
Piercing the tangled foliage through and through,
    With madman gestures uttering scream on scream,
    Dancing like demons in a drunken dream;

How like quick idiots for all the world,
   With sick brains drowned in white fantastic light !
In a wild vortex of light vision whirled,
   They feel a diseased force to mirth incite,
   Fling their swift jokes and laugh with all their might.

See yon old scoundrel, with his snake-like tail
   Securely whipped around his mangrove spar,
Crouched, as I've seen in many an ocean gale,
   Some grimy little shaggy-coated tar,
   High up aloft and peering out afar ;
Mark how he squints at us with ferret eyes,
   Grinning in such a knowing-comic way,
That one would think the wretch malicious wise—
   Or cynic sneering at our lovers' play,
   But start and see how quick he climbs away.

*   *   *   *   *   *   *

The hour of poetry is the hour of morn,
   When up the East the new glad light is breaking,
When songsters rise to greet the day new-born,
   And drowsy plants are from still slumber waking,
   And from their tresses night's pure tear-drops shaking;

When from the azure chambers of the sky
  The gold-haired seraphs throng with airy motion,
To fetch celestial wine of crimson dye
  And sprinkle it upon the face of ocean,
  Where curling lips laugh as they quaff the potion.

Hand me my harp—I'll wake the soul again
  That solaced me in time of bitter woe,
Although I wake it to a sweeter strain
  Than that which swept its wild cords long ago,
  Ere love had taught the minstrel how to glow;
It still perhaps will recognize the hand
  Whose touch called forth its genius so of yore,
Although transplanted from its own stern land
  To sing beside a painted sunshine shore—
  Hail, grand companion! rise and speak once more!

SONG.

DREAMER of the mountain stream,
  Wake thee! wake thee! to my lay!
See! the east is all agleam
  With the rosy flush of day!
Look! the genial god has sprung
  Reddening from the eastern main,
While the ocean's liquid tongue
  Welcomes him to earth again!

Wake thee, dreamer! wake once more,
  From thy long and troubled dream,
Storms and cloudy climes are o'er,
  Wake thee in the tropic beam!
In these richest island bowers,
  In this seat beside the sea,
Languid with the breath of flowers,
  Love is calling low to thee!

Dreamer of the languid eye,
  Rouse thee while I strike the strings!
Sound a sweet glad symphony,
  Made of love's love murmurings;
When thy gush of joy is o'er
  I will hang thee on a tree,
Where the willing winds will pour
  O'er thy soul new melody.

*   *   *   *   *   *   *

Thine eyes, my love, are wells from which I drink
  A more intoxicating wine by half
Than that which sparkles o'er the goblet's brink,
  When gods right merry and right mellow quaff,
  And wake the winking stars with song and laugh

Thy cheeks are like the fig's—but I forbear,
　For want of glowing epithet divine;
For those which paint the charms of other fair
　Are so insipid when applied to thine,
　I cease, and let my silence be their sign.

But love, behold! what tempting treasures lie
　Spread out before us in confusion meet,
Waiting the praise of the delighted eye
　Whose ravished glance they slyly blush to greet,
　Lying so dearly conscious at our feet;
Boy, thou hast done with more than skill thy task,
　(I marvel at such taste in one like thee),
Here is thy gold—nay, take it, and go ask
　Thy dusky mate to join thee 'neath thy tree,
　And lay the yellow pieces on her knee.

Here the dead-ripe bananas are, and here
　The purple figs blush through a cloud of green;
And here the luscious guavas too appear,
　While yonder, peeping from its leafy screen,
　The glorious sapadilla may be seen;
And they that love the kisses of the sun,
　The orange, plantain, and the juicy pine,
Combine their various odors into one

Concentrated breath of luxury divine,
That works upon the sense like mingled wine.

They look too beautiful to mar, and yet
   They are so tempting! come, we'll test their worth!
Ah! here's a draught the gods would not regret—
   Truer than wine and of as choice a birth,
   And freely flows to all alike on earth;
With genial gratitude to Him who fills
   Our arms with gifts on this our holiday,
Partake we of the many things He wills
   His humbler children have without repay,
   So feast and chat the morning hours away.

*   *   *   *   *   *   *

Lo! mark what rare poetic forms obtrude
   To claim the praises of the vagrant gaze,
Bewildered by profusion beauties nude,
   And beauties clothed in bright barbaric blaze
   Some bold, distinct, and some that fade in haze;
The giant cactus, armed in every leaf,
   Stands up defiant, with his single eye
Flaming the vivid passion of a chief
   Upon the humbler beauties standing by,
   Clothed in a rich and humid luxury.

And see how gaily yon ambitious vine
    Has hung his painted pennant from the crest
Of that rude-sculptured pillar-palm of mine—
    The one I chose apart from all the rest
    To guard the entrance of our wildwood nest;
A fancied cord of woven leaves and flowers
    Dropped from the casement of some dwelling-place
Among celestial palaces and towers,
    For fairies weary of the sport and chase
    To mount upon through pathless realms of space.

Like pillars of a massy temple wrought
    And finished with minutest handicraft,
Devices far too infinite for thought,
    To trace the which would turn a mortal daft,
    Dark carvings that on carvings dark engraft;
The stately forest stems in order stand,
    Some bearded with white mosses, some embraced
In the ripe clasp of royal vines in grand
    And rich habiliment, and proudly chaste,
    As warmest trusting maiden undisgraced.

Here life is one long dream voluptuous
    Of softest joys in warm and love-lit ways,
And it is good, for God has willed it thus—
    Secure from peril He has made their days
    Who idle uninquiring through this maze;

But woe to him who reared in sternor clime
   Quits it to find a locked enjoyment here—
To languish 'neath the shade of palm and lime,
   And sip the lotus till his latest year,
   For fiends shall seize him ere his leaf be sear !

But, oh ! to weary mariner what joy
   To see those dark hills rising on his track !
For there he knows the pleasures of the boy,
   E'en though his sun be waning, shall come back
   To rout the thoughts of toil and tempests' rack ;
When close confinement of torturous weeks,
   The master's harsh command and shipmates' growl
Are reckoned with the wind that filled the cheeks
   Of the fat boatswain through the tempest's howl—
   Gone and forgot, like all that blows him foul.

Oh, spot of strange and fatal loveliness,
   No soul is safe beneath thy green arcades !
A peril lurks in every green recess,
   And demons stalk disguised among thy glades,
   To trap the heart that vice in vain invades ;
Thy more than earthly beauty is thy curse,
   And those who yield to it are lost to all—
Lost to life's dear anxieties, and worse,

Lost to the soul's inspiring trumpet-call,
Held satyr-like in nature's sensuous thrall.

*　　*　　*　　*　　*　　*　　*

Soon I must turn me toward that stormy land
　　Where pure Lake George's crystal waters lie
Asleep in hills magnificent and grand,
　　Eternal guardians of their chastity,
　　Looking forever on them from on high;
Must shake me from these sea's embracing arms,
　　Where I have lived a wrapt delightful dream,
To seek 'mong hardier scenes and homelier charms
　　The hidden fountain of contentment's stream,
　　While youth and love yet shed a magic beam.

And thou, my love, shalt be a star to light
　　A lovely beacon on these noble hills,
Where moons flash cold along the snow-robed height,
　　And skies weep frozen tears, and tardy rills
　　Are caught and prisoned in a wall that chills;
Chills their light singing hearts, and prisoned long,
　　Mourn deep down in their bosoms for release,
Till youthful spring comes dancing in with song,
　　And wealth of hope and passion and increase
　　To melt their bonds and let them go in peace.

So we have talked and feasted till the sun
   In his proud station in the middle sky,
Rejoices at the height that he has won
   Above the glories that beneath him lie,
   Glad in the fire of his benignant eye;
And now our sweet siesta will we take,
   From his hot glance so slyly hid away—
But stop! once more the charm of song I'll wake,
   Ere our blithe spirits leave the brilliant day,
   Among the flowery paths of sleep to stray.

SONG.

   SLEEP, my bride, in slumber fair,
   Olive shades are in thy hair;
   On thy cheeks in brown disguise
   Are the tints of southern skies;
      Tropic loves are slyly hid
      Underneath each pearly lid,

   Fays that lurk in orange bloom,
   Blending with luxuriant gloom,
      Hover o'er in fairy glee
      At their glad discovery,
   Longing for a kiss, but shy,
   Lest the darling wake and fly.

Sleep and dream on balmy bed
Of the joys that we have wed ;
Sleep and dream, and have no fear,
Love will guard thy pillow, dear ;
But when sleep withdraws his charms,
Waken, dreamer, to my arms !

III.

SEA MUSIC.

Songs of the sea ! can I resist the spell
Which their old lonely prophecies have wrought
Upon my saddened spirits ?   Can I quell
Those sole inspirers of my drooping thought,
And set their solemn warnings all at naught ?
Can I forego that deep enjoyment now
The only rapture that my soul can grasp,
My heart assimilate, my mind avow—
That friend who holds me with close careful clasp
Back from the brink of silence where I gasp ?

Songs of the sea! breathings of the immense,
   Steadily sounding through the hollow years
That rise to smother them, what joy intense
   Works up this settled sediment of tears
   Choked down, when they come chanting in my ears;
Oh, while I scale this old and crumbling wall,
   Slipping and stumbling o'er the loosened stones,
Painfully guarding 'gainst a fatal fall,
   Bravely I'll hail the pleasure that atones·
   For 'periled soul sustained 'midst throes and groans!

Songs of the sea! what witching numbers flow
   With the full stream of their divinest strain!
Filling the endless epic with the glow
   That stings the bosom with delicious pain,
   Sweet mysteries that plague me not in vain;
Wonderful melodies that in my ears
   Are ever ringing, though far, far away
From Father Ocean my lost vessel steers—
   In vain I climb my cliffs, in vain essay
   Life's common course, they chain—charm me alway!

Songs of the sea—hush! they are on me now—
   Do you not see their shadow in my eyes?
Do you not see the mystery on my brow—
   The vague mist of perplexity that lies
   Upon it like a thin cloud on the skies?

You speak and I but hear you in a dream,
   You laugh and your vain mirth sounds faint and far,
My old sad soul is where white whirlpools gleam,
   Where yellow typhoons wheel the blazing car,
   And tempests stalk 'midst flame and thunder-jars.

IV.

WEAVING.

In this odd brain of mine there seems to be
   A loom whose noiseless shuttles night and day
Are busy with the threads of memory,
   Weaving of tangled ends so all astray
   A gauzy garment, various and gay ;
A secret swift machine that works by stealth
   This wonder-wrought poetic cloth-of-gold,
Dearer to me than heaps of golden wealth
   Piled higher than the pyramids of old,
   Or treasures that beneath the sea shine cold.

Set in the waves that around me float and flow,
   And shift and glitter, with delight I view
As in the texture of a shifting shore,
   Past thoughts of every lovely shape and hue
   Worked in and blended marvelously true ;

How strange! with what amused perplexity
    I strive to read the inextricable sign!
The characters are so complex to me—
    So mixed and intermingled line in line,
    I cease, and cry impatient " 'Tis divine!"

V.

A RAGE.

OPE wide thy awful armed mouth, O sea,
    And roar and bellow till the big earth quake
In fear and terror, and then scornfully
    Spit full upon her face, and beat and shake
    Her dry old carcass till the dead awake;
Dip thy long fingers down into the slime,
    And rake up all the bodies of thy dead
And build thyself a wall no man can climb—
    A barrier 'twixt thee and a race whose tread
    Would brand with shame thy gray and honored head!

Yea, frighten and appall him, wall him in,
    Seize on and shake him, crush him in thy hold,
And overwhelm and craze him with thy din,
    Or he will turn thy waters into gold,
    And part thee piecemeal as his soul he sold;

Concentrate all thy strength into one blow,
   And sweep his monstrous sodoms from thy breast—
These dens of evil passing to and fro
   Beneath the shadow of the eagle's crest,
   Vile blots upon God's noblest works and best

SEA SONGS.

SEA DREAM.

THEY told me of an isle upon the deep
   Broad bosom of a far unfathomed sea,
Where, in the blest serenity of sleep,
   Fed by bright visions lay sweet Poesy.

They told me in a thrilling whisper how,
   Lured by some captive spirit of the sky,
A few fond ones had stolen from his brow
   Some glorious leaves of immortality.

How they abandoned in mid sea the craft
   Which erst their daily care it was to guide,
And stretched away where new waves danced and
     laughed
   In fairy shell-boat o'er an unknown tide.

They hinted, too, of perils and of straits—
  Of rocks and whirlpools feared and tempted long;
The fair false beacons of wild wrecker hates,
  And sweet temptation's haunting siren-song.

They pictured then in colors like the sun
  A bright isle swimming in a crimson haze;
Unfolding all its beauties one by one,
  They spread them out before my ravished gaze.

Such loveliness as tongue cannot report
  Dawned slow revealed on my untrammeled sight,
Such scenes as fancy in her wildest sport
  Ne'er furnished forth to dazzle and delight.

"This is the region of perpetual youth,
  For which so many struggle, few attain,
Here only those who dare to know the truth
  Awake the harp to an undying strain.

" Only the intrepid ones who dare to quaff
  The draught of maddening knowledge, dregs of earth,
And hold aloft the empty cup and laugh
  Fulfill the glory of a poet's birth.

" 'Neath the deceitful quiet of these waves
  Lie hid the demon guardians of the land;
Woe, want, misfortune, lurk where countless graves
  Lie strewn along ocean's glittering sand.

" *They* are the potent powers that ever haunt
  The unguarded footsteps of the son of song,
They wield the scourges formed to disenchant
  His habitation of its airy throng!

" Whirled in the vortex of terrestrial fears,
  Beholding giant shadows veil their skies,
Thousands have crowned with folly all their years.
  Or died with glory dawning on their eyes.

" Or eager for a fruit so long withheld
  Have stooped to pluck its semblance by the way,
And yielding where its subtle power impelled,
  Lost hope forever by their fond delay.

" Not theirs the sturdy hearts designed to bear
  Unbroke the ills that prey upon mankind;
Hate spread his dire enchantments from his lair
  And smote the unstable fabric of the mind.

" Oh, thou who feel'st within thy breast the sting
  Of precious pains dealt by no mortal hand!
If thou wouldst stretch away on boundless wing
  To win the treasures of that matchless land—

" If thou wouldst reach secure this isle of fame,
  Live in earth's love, wring from its misery
Those priceless drops which feed the sacred flame
  Upon the altar of humanity ! "

The wondrous music ceased, and I awoke
  To see the bright dawn break o'er coral isles;
And ocean, throwing off his cloudy cloak,
  Leap laughing forth to meet her maiden smiles.

ROVER'S LOVE SONG.

DEAR stranger, wheresoe'er thou art,
  That crosses thus a wanderer's way,
Thy wondrous eyes have found my heart
  And left therein a deathless ray!

A deathless ray, and oh, so sweet!
  And now the star to guide me on;
Above the storm's confused retreat
  I see a port that may be won.

The lamp that guided me for years
  Has sunk beneath the solemn sea,
And on the horizon appears
  A prophet star of hope for me.

And chains that fettered me to woe
  Have fallen, and behind me lie,
Their deadening gall no more I know—
  Thy magic chain their place supply.

Thy fairy form, thy angel face,
  The marvel of thine eyes, and all,
Combine to form that nameless grace
  Which doth my every sense enthrall.

Sweet bondage! happy captive, I,
  In such immortal bonds to serve—
I sigh and look, and look and sigh,
  While boundless love thrills every nerve!

One kiss from those red lips of thine—
  Away! I must but look and sigh,
The thought is like forbidden wine,
  Which burns but cannot satisfy!

Mine is the first fierce love of youth—
  Life's highest, truest ecstacy,
A spark of that divinest truth
  Which burns through all eternity.

We have not spoken—words of mine
  Could never half this heart reveal;
Thou'st read my soul as I have thine—
  Enough! we know what each must feel.

And so through all the tropic day,
  And while night sleeps upon the sea,
I'll let my sail drift on its way,
  And dream of happiness and thee.

A SEA SONG.

THE main! the main! the Spanish Main!
I'm on the boundless wave again!
  I feel my pulses wildly thrill,
  A frenzied joy my senses fil!,
The wave that bears me bounds less free
Than my heart in its ecstacy!

I live! I breathe! I burn! I flame—
I have a bliss I cannot name!
  The essence of a fiercer soul
  Leaps through my blood without control,
The spirits of the sea and sky
Are reveling with my fantasy!

I wake as from a torpid sleep
To feel the wave beneath me leap,
  To see the airy cloudlet driven
  Across the blue expanse of heaven,
And know the breeze that fans my brow
Is wafting me from madness now.

The main! the main! the joyous main!
The world of wonders! I would fain

Forever guide my little sail
Before its balm-redolent gale,
And on, and on, forever free—
A thing without a destiny!

My bride no mortal maid shall be,
I'll wed alone the sea! the sea!
   Though treacherous her breast may seem,
   It holds a wild and thrilling dream,
It holds a glorious mystery—
A sweet and new eternity.

AN INVOCATION.

Come, child of might,
   From the storm-chambers of the painted west,
Come with thy torch plucked from the towers of night,
   And fire this breast!

Come, while the sea,
   Touched by the gray look of expiring day,
Sounds from his deep-toned harp in sympathy
   A farewell lay!

Not like the breath
    Of the soft zephyr stealing o'er the sea,
Nor like the silent step of gentle death,
    Come thou to me.

Nor like the flight
    Of the pure white-winged messenger of peace,
Nor the sweet stealth of wedded love at night,
    With fond disease

Not thus of yore
    To the earth's darlings wert thou wont to steal,
But midst the rack of tempests, and the roar
    Of whirlwind's reel!

Come with the charge
    Of the strong warriors of the upper deep,
And rouse my languid spirit from the marge
    Of loathsome sleep.

Come like the flight
    Of the bold sea bird beautiful and free,
Laden with treasures from the Infinite,
    Come thou to me!

Come, loved of God,
    To this low valley in the realm of years!
Come oft to cheer us in our sad abode
    Of hopes and fears!

PORT ROYAL.

I REST me where for ages the old years
   Have hung their shaggy beards upon the oaks—
The hoary honors of departed seers,
   Which playful zephyrs smooth with gentle strokes,
   And pull about with whispered laughs and jokes!
I watch with eyes half closed in dreamy ease
   The smoke go curling up from my cigar,
And wind like chains of phantoms 'mong the trees,
   Until they seem as infinitely far
   As telescopic creatures of a star.

How sweet the breezy calm of this retreat
   After so many years of ocean's din!
How strange to feel the firm sod 'neath my feet
   Instead of quaking timbers toiling in
   A tumbled mass of waves that reel and spin!
Ah, how delightful to behold on high
   The green of nature, 'stead of hollow sails
Like wings of some great bird outstretched to fly
   Afar o'er ocean's shifting hills and vales—
   My heart bursts wide its doors, and peace prevails!

Peace! what a mighty meaning in the word,
  For one whose days were one continued strain
Of closest contest with the foes that stirred
  To hot rebellion this combative brain,
  Though they assailed the loyal heart in vain!
So new—so foreign the transition seems,
  I start and pass my hand across my brow,
Where blended memories lie dim like dreams,
  And question when I died, and where, and how,
  And is this paradise that I see now.

The streams slip by upon their winding ways
  Among the shrubs and grasses, while the lines
Of giant stems stand up as if to gaze
  Upon their pictures, framed in curling vines,
  Within the liquid mirror oaks and pines—
Rough-sculptured columns of this vast arcade,
  Whose one roof arches upward high and cool,
Mapped with a hundred landscapes, where light shades
  Come first and dance like shadows on a pool,
  With noises like the bees in busy school.

A score of winged embodied melodies
  Fall fluttering down around me without fear,
And peep at me with sweet and funny eyes,
  Singing as if to hail my presence here,
  Brimful of fairy joy and wildwood cheer;

The epicurean squirrel up aloft,
  The refuse of his feast drops in my face,
And chuckles with a mirth full sly and soft,
  Then climbs away with swift and nimble pace,
  Amused at his own wit and my disgrace.

The bees grope blindly among the flowers and moss,
  In search of sweets deep hidden from the day—
Feel in and out, and creep and crawl across
  The hearts of stately plants, then reel away,
  Like little drunkards trying to be gay;
While countless winged creatures swim about
  In the thin rivers of the atmosphere
Shot through and through with sunbeams, in and out,
  Like counter rays they dart, their fleet career
  Flashing bright sparkles down the currents clear.

Behind me lies the ocean's lonely waste,
  Dim with the years that I've thrown overboard—
The rinds of fruit once pleasant to my taste,
  But I have sucked their sweetness—I have cored
  Their hearts of that which lay within them stored;
Drawn them as you would draw an orange dry
  And fling the dead and shrivelled skin away,
To grasp a larger riper one; thus I
  Turn from the dead unto the living day,
  And pluck the good of life ere its decay.

Before me coils a circle of blue hills,
  Whose blackened bones show through their tattered
    cloaks
The winds attempt to mend ; at intervals
  Out from their bosoms drift tall ships of smoke,
  With guns athunder, scarred and battle-broke ;
And looming near discover to my gaze
  The placid features of each passive crew
Looking and smiling on me through the haze,
  That warms their features with a sunset hue—
  When lo ! they are long wished for friends I view !

Thus sally forth the loving hearts of home
  To find me resting in this border land,
Between the barbarous ocean with his foam,
  And that calm region stretching me a hand,
  Where culture smiles, and genial arts expand ;
Lo ! I will shake the sea-dust from my locks,
  Uncoil the sea-knots that enthrall my tongue,
And hie me to that dear nook 'mong the rocks,
  Where oft the crazy cataract has sung
  My poet heart to rest when passion-strung.

VALE.

BLOW soft, O winds, along the southern sea;
   Sing low, O sea, your wildest, sweetest song—
Sad, like the one with which you welcomed me
   When first I rested on thy bosom strong,
   A homeless wanderer fleeing from my wrong;
When from my woe and sin I shook me clear,
   And came and poured my sorrows on your breast;
For unto me you have been very dear,
   E'en in your rages, yielding me a rest,
   A balm, a peace, a love the tenderest!

Then winds, blow soft, and sea, sing low and wild,
   Once more before I speak my last farewell,
Depart a man, who sought you as a child,
   Changed by the soothing magic of your spell,
   Taught how to labor and to combat well;
Perhaps that after years your thrilling voice
   Will reach me in my mountain solitude;
Then, if my heart has wearied of its choice,
   And pineth like a sea-bird tamely mewed
   I'll fly to you and have my joy renewed.

THE END.

Evolution and Progress:

An Exposition and Defence. The Foundation of Evolution Philosophically Expounded, and its Arguments (divested of insignificant and distracting physical details) succinctly stated; together with a review of leading opponents, as Dawson and Winchell, and quasi-opponents, as Le Conte and Carpenter. By Rev. WILLIAM I. GILL, A. M., of Newark Conference, N. J. *The first volume of the International Prize Series.* THIRD EDITION. Cloth extra, imitation morocco, fine paper, 295 pp., 12mo., Price . $1 50

Each volume in this series was awarded a prize of *Two Hundred Dollars* in addition to copyright, in a competition which was open one year to the world, and where over three hundred manuscripts were submitted and read.

Analytical Processes;

Or, The Primary Principle of Philosophy. By REV. WILLIAM I. GILL. A. M., author of "Evolution and Progress." *The Third Volume of the International Prize Series.* Cloth extra, fine paper, uniform with "Evolution and Progress," 450 pp., 12mo. Price $2 00.

A work which the committee cannot describe without seeming to exaggerate. It is marked by extraordinary depth and originality, and yet it is so clear and convincing as to make its novel conclusions appear like familiar common sense.—*From Report of Committee of Prize Award.*

It contains a vast amount of able and conscientious thought and acute criticism.—*Dr. McCosh, Prest. Princeton College.*

A specimen of robust thinking. I am very much gratified with its thoroughness, acuteness and logical coherence.—*Dr. Anderson, Pres't Rochester University.*

Ecclesiology:

A Fresh Inquiry as to the Fundamental Idea and Constitution of the New Testament Church; with a Supplement on Ordination. By REV. E. J. FISH, D. D. Cloth extra, fine paper, 400 pp., 12mo. . Price $2 00.

DOCTOR FISH disposes this volume into four parts.—I. The Fundamental Idea of the Church; II. The New Testament Church Constitution; III. Application of Principles; IV. A Supplement on Ordination—and addresses himself to his themes with the full earnestness of ability, clearness of logic, and conscientiousness or spirit which comprehensive treatment requires. As a "building fitly framed together," it is a fair-minded and standard contribution to the best religious literature of the Christian age.

The Beauty of the King:

By REV. A. H. HOLLOWAY, A. M., author of "Good Words for S. S. Teachers," "Teachers' Meetings," etc. Cloth extra, 174 pp. 12mo, $1.00; full gilt, beveled edges, $1.25.

A remarkably clear, comprehensive and intelligible exposition of the natural and spiritual causes, processes and effects of the birth, life and death of Jesus—a subject much discussed, yet not generally understood now-a-days.

Life for a Look:

By REV. A. H. HOLLOWAY, A. M. Paper covers, 32mo.
Price, 15 cts.

Earnest, cogent words, marrowy with the spirit of honest, old-fashioned Religion.

Is Our Republic a Failure?

A discussion of the Rights and the Wrongs of the North and the South. By E. H. WATSON, author of "United States and their Origin," etc. English cloth, ink and gold, 12mo, 436 pp. . . . . Price, $1.50

In a spirit of genuine candor and unswerving impartiality.—*N. Y. Sun.*

It is fair, candid, impartial, the whole subject well treated.—Hon. J. H BLAKE, *of Boston.*

I like the spirit of the book, its comprehensive patriotism, its liberal spirit, and its healing counsels.—Hon. GEO. S. HILLARD, *author of " Franklin Readers," " Six Months in Italy,"* etc.

I read the manuscript with much interest—an interest belonging to the arguments themselves, but now increased by the perfection given to the form and style.—Hon. MARTIN BRIMMER, *Boston.*

Lucid and just. The method of the argument, the facts on which it proceeds, and the conciliatory spirit which invests them, contribute to the book a value which cannot be too highly estimated.—GEN. JOHN COCHRANE.

The principles of American statesmanship which it asserts, must essentially prevail, unless we are so soon to fall from our original high plane of constitutional republicanism. I shall spare no exertion to promote the knowledge of such an able and impartial and statesmanlike compendium of our present political philosophy.—Hon. JOHN QUINCY ADAMS, *Mass.*

Clearly expressed, and the argument is closely and ably maintained. The tone and the temper of the writer are beyond praise. They are as valuable as they are rare. They are those of a patriotic and philosophical observer of men. The like spirit everywhere diffused among our people would make fraternal union as certain as desirable ; and if brought to the discussion of public affairs, would secure the adoption of wise and beneficent, counsels.—Hon. GEO. H. PENDLETON, *Ohio.*

Universe of Language.

I.—ITS NATURE. II.—STRUCTURE. III.—SPELLING REFORM Comprising Uniform Notation and Classification of Vowels adapted to all Languages. By the late GEORGE WATSON, Esq., of Boston. Edited, with Preliminary Essays, and a Treatise on Phonology, Phonotypy and Spelling Reform, by his daughter, E. H. WATSON, author of "Is Our Republic a Failure?" etc. Cloth extra, tinted paper, 12mo, 344 pp. Price $1.50

One of the great scientific labors of Mr. Watson's life was to segregate and systematize the universal elements of Language. His investigations were broad and comprehensive. Miss Watson has rounded her father's work with worthy zeal and eminent ability ; and the result, in this volume, is a unique and learned contribution to the permanent advantage and advancement of philology.

Christian Conception and Experience.

By Rev. WM. I. GILL, A. M., author of "Evolution and Progress," "Analytical Processes," etc. Imitation Morocco 12mo. . . . . Price, $1 00.

A fresh exposition and argument, practically enforced by a remarkable narrative of the conversion of a skeptic through this same argument. While it exhibits in parts the philosophic cast of the author's mind, its vivacious and lucid treatment will create for it a universal interest. This third work—in order of publication—by this fearless investigator, has, in large part, been written since his Trial before the Newark Methodist Episcopal Conference, under the charge of "Heresy," for writing his EVOLUTION AND PROGRESS, and it supplies abundant, fresh and vigorous thought-pabulum for the entertainment of heretics, critics, and Christians alike.

Resurrection of the Body. Does the Bible Teach it?

By E. NISBET, D. D. With an Introduction by G. W. SAMSON, D. D., late President of Columbian University, D. C. Fine English cloth, 12mo. Price $1.00.

This is the careful work of an independent thinker and bold investigator. He strips away the trammels of hereditary prejudice, breaks the "old bottles" of unreasoning bias, and, with invincible logic, enters a field of research which had almost made a coward of thought. He begs no questions, makes no special pleadings, but meets the issue in its full front with such clean honesty and consummate ability that the book will interest and instruct every fair-minded reader, and charm and gratify every earnest student.

Reverend Green Willingwood;

Or, LIFE AMONG THE CLERGY. By Rev. ROBERT FISHER. Silk cloth, ink and gold, beveled edges, full gilt. 12mo, $1.25.

With a resolute spirit and a knightly lance the Rev. Green Willingwood fights the battles of his brother clergymen. His battle ground is in the midst of every congregation. His armament is comprised of faithful work, hearty humor and delicate satire. In short, Rev. Green Willingwood says and does precisely that which is wont to be said and done, but which, for obvious reasons, cannot be spoken from the pulpit nor accomplished directly in the pastorate.

Deacon Cranky.

By GEORGE GUIREY. Cloth extra, clear type. Price.. $1.50

A bright and vigorous story in which every reader will readily recognize the familiar form of Deacon Cranky, whose strong points are superbly developed by Church Fairs, Choir troubles, Charity Contributions, Dorcas Society missions, religious Sleigh-rides and moral Necktie Parties, while the thread of the story retains vital earnestness, sharp characterization, and absorbing interest throughout.

PRACTICAL THOUGHT.

Mercantile Prices and Profits;

Or the Valuation of Commodities for a Fair Trade. By M. R. PILON. Handsomely printed, 8vo., paper, 100 pp., ... In Press.

The author has brought broad experience and comprehensive research to bear upon his subjects. His style is terse and perspicuous. He uses the easy and concise language of an educated business man; and, with wonderful art, invests every chapter with the grace and charm of a well-told story.

Monetary Feasts and Famines;

Labor, Values, Prices, Foreign and Fair Trade, Scarcity of Money and the Causes of Inflation. By M. R. PILON, author of "The Grangers." Uniform with "The Grangers,"—(In Press.) . .

What is Demonetization?

Ways to arrive at the Demonetization of Gold and Silver, and the establishment of Private Banks under control of the National Government. By. M. R. PILON, author of "The Grangers." FIFTH EDITION. 8vo., 186 pp., paper cover, . . Price 75 cents.

The work is interesting, and especially valuable to financiers.—*Jersey City Daily Journal*.

He gives expression to a good deal of sound financial principle.—*Louisville Daily Commercial*.

It is full of common sense......Valuable for its facts, its thoughts and its suggestions.—*Troy Daily Whig*.

Is written in an interesting and popular style and contains much useful information.—*Oakland, Cal., Daily News*.

The subject of the high valuation of gold and silver currency is fully discussed, and offers some new ideas worthy the attention of those interested in monetary affairs.—*Toledo Commercial*.

The author is a merchant who has extensively studied the currency problem. His hits are often sharp and incisive........Mr. Pilon would provide ample banking facilities for every city, town and village, with both stock and land security.—*Cincinnati Daily Star*.

........Discussing the currency question in an original, forcible and entertaining style. The author has brought together a great amount of varied information upon the whole subject of money......Those interested will find unquestioned ability in the author's handling of it.—*Baltimore Methodist Protestant*.

The Manuscript Manual:

How to Prepare Manuscripts for the Press—practical and to the point. Paper, 26 pp., 8vo. Price 10 cents.

A most useful little companion to the young writer and editor.—*The South, New York*.

Gives excellent hints to intending writers.—*Cleveland Evan. Messenger*

The Race for Wealth,

Considered in a Series of Letters written to each other by a Brother and Sister. Edited by JAMES CORLEY. 12mo, 180 pp., paper . . . . . . Price 50 cents.

Shows how labor strikes may be prevented; how women may advance their political influence; how marriage may recover due regard in public opinion; the impossibility of enforcing total abstinence from strong liquors; and treats these and other topics of social and political economy in a clear style, making the work peculiarly attractive and impressive.

Aptly considered.—*St. Louis Christian.*
Of special importance.—*Cincinnati Gazette.*
Attractive . . . needed.—*Quincy Whig.*
Sensible, robust, sound.—*Hartford Courant.*
Clear, earnest, thoughtful.—*Phila. Nat. Baptist.*
Pleasant, intelligent, wholesome, useful.—*Zion's Herald, Boston.*
Simplicity in the arguments and the way of presenting them that is refreshing.—*Louisville Courier Journal.*

Author's Manuscript Paper.

Made from superior stock, in two grades, and sold only in ream packages. Each package warranted to contain full count of 480 sheets.

MANUFACTURED BY THE AUTHORS' PUBLISHING COMPANY.

AUTHOR'S MANUSCRIPT PAPER, 5¾ + 11, per ream . . . $1.00
AUTHOR'S MANUSCRIPT PAPER, 5¾ + 11, heavier, per ream . 1.25

NOTE.—When paper is sent by mail 50 cents per ream, in addition to price, must accompany order, to prepay postage.

It is only by making a specialty of this paper, manufacturing directly at the mills in large quantities, and selling exclusively for cash, that the demand can be supplied at these low prices. It is really nearly ONE HUNDRED PER CENT. cheaper than any other paper in the market.

It is ruled on one side, the other plain; is approved by writers and preferred by printers; and it has now become the popular standard paper for authors, contributors, editors, and writers generally.

☞ The A. P. Co. sell no other stationery.

A very convenient size, and at a low price.—*Publishers' Weekly, N. Y.*

The distinguishing feature of the Manuscript Paper is its convenient shape. The texture is neither too thick nor too thin, making it in every way a desirable paper for writers and contributors.—*Acta Columbiana, New York.*

It is especially useful for writers for the press, combining as it does good quality with cheapness. The convenience of form is apparent to all who have writing to do, while it soon saves its price in postage.—*Essex County Press, Newark, N. J.*

Thousands of letters from well known authors, editors, and writers are on file in our office expressing the highest satisfaction with this paper, and thanking us for introducing it into market.

ÆSTHETIC THOUGHT.

Irene; or, Beach-Broken Billows:

A Story. By Mrs. B. F. BAER, author of "Lena's Marriage," "The Match-Girl of New York," "Little Bare-Foot," etc., etc. *The second volume of the International Prize Series.* SECOND EDITION. Cloth extra, fine thick paper. 12mo. . . . Price $1 00.

Natural, honest and delicate.—*New York Herald.*
Charming and thoughtful.—*Poughkeepsie Eagle.*
Depicted in strong terms.—*Baptist Union, New York.*
Eminently pleasing and profitable.—*Christian Era, Boston.*
A fascinating volume.—*Georgia Musical Eclectic Magazine.*
Characters and plot fresh and original.—*Bridgeport News.*
With freshness, clearness, and vigor.—*Neb. Watchman.*
Delightful book.—*Saturday Review, Louisville, Ky.*
Lays open a whole network of the tender and emotional.—*Williamsport (Pa.) Daily Register.*
The unity is well preserved, the characters maintaining that probability so essential in the higher forms of fiction.—*Baltimore Methodist Protestant.*
There is a peculiar charm in the reading of this book, which every one who peruses it must feel. It is very like to that which is inspired in reading any of Hawthorne's romances.—*Hartford Religious Herald.*

Wild Flowers:

Poems. By CHARLES W. HUBNER, author of "Souvenirs of Luther." Elegantly printed on fine tinted paper, with portrait of the Author, imitation morocco and beveled edges, 196 pp., 12mo. *Just ready,*

Price $1.00. The same, gilt top, beveled edges, **$1.25**

As a poet Mr. HUBNER is conservative—always tender and delicate, never turbid or erratic. He evinces a strong love of nature and high spirituality, and brings us, from the humblest places and in the humblest guises, beauties of the heart, the life, the universe, and, while placing them before our vision, has glorified them and shown that within them of whose existence we had never dreamed.

Her Waiting Heart:

A Novel. By LOU CAPSADELL, author of "Hallow E'en." Cloth extra, 192 pp., 12mo. *Just ready.* $1 00.
A story of New York—drawn from the familiar phases of life, which, under the calmest surfaces, cover the greatest depths. Charming skill is shown in the naturalness of characterization, development of plot and narrative, strength of action and delicacy of thought.

Women's Secrets; or, How to be Beautiful:

Translated and Edited from the Persian and French, with additions from the best English authorities. By Loc. CAPSADELL, author of "Her Waiting Heart," "Hallow E'en," etc. Pp. 100, 12mo.

Saratoga Edition, in Scotch granite paper covers, 25 cents.

Boudoir Edition, French grey and blue cloths, . 75 cents.

The systems, directions and recipes for promoting Personal Beauty, as practiced for thousands of years by the renowned beauties of the Orient, and for securing the grace and charm for which the French Toilette and Boudoir are distinguished, together with suggestions from the best authorities, comprising History and Uses of Beauty; The Best Standards; Beautiful Children; Beauty Food, Sleep, Exercise, Health, Emotions· How to be Fat; How to be Lean; How to be Beautiful and to remain so, etc., etc.

Sumners' Poems:

By SAMUEL B. SUMNER and CHARLES A. SUMNER. With Illustrations by E. STEWART SUMNER. On fine tinted paper, 518 pp., cloth extra. Regular 12mo edition, $2.50 Large paper, 8vo, illustrated, full gilt, beveled edges...$4.00

Sparkling, tender and ardent.—*Philadelphia Book Buyer.*
Vivacity and good humor.—DR. OLIVER WENDELL HOLMES.
Brilliant and humorous, patriotic and historic.—*American Monthly, Phila.*
Equal to anything that is at all akin to them in "The Excursion."—*N. Y. World.*

The Buccaneers:

A stirring Historical Novel. By RANDOLPH JONES, Esq. Large 12mo, cloth extra, ink and gold. Paper $1. Cloth $1.75.

Is drawn from the most daring deeds of the Buccaneers and the sharpest events in the early settlement of Maryland and Virginia. It is so full of thrilling action, so piquant in sentiment, and so thoroughly alive with the animation of the bold and ambitious spirits whose acts it records with extraordinary power, that the publishers confidently bespeak "THE BUCCANEERS" as the most strongly marked and the best of all American novels issued during the year.

Cothurnus and Lyre.

By EDWARD J. HARDING. Fine English cloth, ink and gold, 12mo, 126 pp.... .... $1 00

Real poetic feeling and power.—*Am. Bookseller.*
Nobility not without sweetness.—*N. Y. World.*
Vigor which is quite uncommon.—*London Spectator.*
A unique and striking work.—*Boston Home Journal.*
Models of neatness and consideration.—*N. Y. Commercial.*
Has created a sensation in Eastern literary circles.—*Chicago Herald.*

THE SATCHEL SERIES.—NOTICE.

This popular series comprises the brightest and best brief works of fiction by AMERICAN AUTHORS who are, for the most part, well known to the reading public. They are not trashy reprints nor dime novels. They are clean and polished in matter, printed in large type, bound in convenient shape, and offer fascinating and delightful reading alike for RAILWAY, FIRESIDE and LIBRARY.

Lily's Lover; or, a Trip Out of Season.

By the author of "Climbing the Mountains," etc. Satchel Series; square 12mo, paper covers .   .   . 35 cents.

A very sweet and pretty story of summer-time romantic adventures among the green hills and silvery lakes of Connecticut.

Rosamond Howard.

By KATE R. LOVELACE. Satchel Series; square 12mo, paper covers .   .   .   .   . 25 cents.
Extra edition, in fine English cloth .   .   60 "

A quiet, pathetic and attractive story, excellently managed and beautifully told, with continuous and increasing interest.

The Voice of a Shell.

By O. C. AURINGER. Satchel Series; square 12mo, paper covers .   .   .   . 50 cents.

To all lovers of the sea, and to all who linger by its sounding shores, nothing can be more entrancing than the pages of this beautiful little volume. It is delicate, brilliant and grand.

Shadowed Perils:

A Novel. By M. A. AVERY, author of "The Loyal
Bride," etc. English cloth, 260 pp., 12mo, . . . $1 00

The story is bold and dramatic in action, graceful in narrative, strong in characterization, intense in interest, sweet and pure in tone, and is marked by keen sympathy with
the lowly and oppressed.

Prisons Without Walls (Satchel Series):

A Novel. By KELSIC ETHERIDGE. Paper, ˙ pp.,
Price, 35 cents.

Has the curiosity-exciting tendency.—*Boston Beacon.*

The interest grows and retains attention to the end.—*N. O. Picayune.*

Short, sententious, marrowy, and spiced with episodes. Has a warm southern aroma
of orange and magnolia blossoms.—*Baltimore Meth. Prot.*

Of rare beauty and power in its vivid, life-like picturing of men and places . . . . . .
Through such artistic touches of skill and strength we are wafted in thought as we follow the hero and heroine through the mazes of the old, old story.—*Ladies' Pearl, St. Louis.*

The Travelers' Grab-Bag; or, the Heart of a Quiet Hour:
(Satchel Series.)

A Hand-book for utilizing fragments of leisure in railroad
trains, steamboats, way stations and easy chairs. Edited
by AN OLD TRAVELER. . . . Paper, ·· pp.,
Price, 35 cents.

Full of spice and fun.—*Baltimore Meth. Prot.*

No traveler should be without it.—*N. Y. Forest and Stream.*

Teeming with rollicking humor and a kind of satire that will be enjoyable.—*Pittsburgh
Commercial.*

Bonny Eagle. (Satchel Series.)

Clear type, heavy tinted paper, 12mo, . . 25 cents.
The curious and ludicrous experiences of a party of gentlemen who
sought happiness in the forests of Maine; graphically told with a naive
humor and delicate satire; fresh and spicy.

Nobody's Business.

SATCHEL SERIES. BY JEANNETTE R. HADERMANN, author of "Dead Men's Shoes," "Heavy Yokes," "Against the World," etc. Square 12mo, 128 pp., paper. . . 30 cents.

An admirable book.—*Phila. Record.*
A charming book.—*Phila. Edit. of Literature.*
Full of lively sallies and bright hits.—*Bap. Weekly, N. Y.*
A sprightly, capitally told narrative—sympathetically interesting and highly amusing.—*Boston Home Journal.*
A rollicking, breezy tale. A more charming book, for sheer amusement, we have seldom met with.—*N. Y. Mail.*
Affords more hearty laughs than can be gotten out of the best comic play. The style is polished and spirited, the wit piquant, and its common sense sound as a dollar.—*Vicksburg Herald.*

Our Winter Eden.

PEN PICTURES OF THE TROPICS, with an Appendix of the SEWARD-SAMANA MYSTERY. By Mrs. W. L. CAZNEAU, author of "Prince Kashna," "Eagle Pass," "Hill Homes of Jamaica." SATCHEL SERIES. Square 12mo., 130 pp., paper. . . . . 30 cents.

Mrs. Cazneau has resided, during the winters of twenty years, amidst the scenes of which she writes. General Cazneau being for many years the Commissioner from the United States to Santo Domingo. The author imparts to her Pen Pictures the very glow of that soft climate which " has no winter in its year." She captures every sense with panoramic descriptions of enchanting landscapes, glowing with rich tints and breathing the sweet fragrance of rosy June.

An Earnest Appeal to Moody.

A SATIRE. SATCHEL SERIES. Square 12mo, 34 pp., paper, ... 10 cents.

A stinging thrust at some of the foibles of Newspaper Row and Brooklyn's political rings. The performance is bright, pointed and keen.

The hits are well taken and to the point, and will be appreciated by many, as the names are outlined sufficiently to be readily recognized.—*Edit. of Literature, Phila.*
The references to —— —— —— and the rest will prove quite amusing, especially as this satire represents them as amenable to reform and to be conscience-stricken by Mr. Moody's preaching.—*Brooklyn Times.*

A Story of the Strike.

SCENES IN CITY LIFE. SATCHEL SERIES. BY ELIZABETH MURRAY. Illustrated. Square 12mo, 128 pages. . 30 cents.

Vivacious tale.—*N. Y. Mail.*
Is a pretty story.—*N. Y. Eve. Telegram.*
Characters are well drawn.—*St. Louis Herald.*
A pleasant story.—*Sunday School Times.*
Is a beautiful story.—*Boston Home Journal.*
Will amuse the family circle.—*Kansas City Times.*